The Liberal Arts College Adapting to Change

GARLAND STUDIES IN HIGHER EDUCATION
VOLUME 9
GARLAND REFERENCE LIBRARY OF SOCIAL SCIENCE
VOLUME 1011

GARLAND STUDIES IN HIGHER EDUCATION

This series is published in cooperation with the Program in Higher Education, School of Education, Boston College, Chestnut Hill, Massachusetts.

PHILIP G. ALTBACH, *Series Editor*

THE SOCIAL ROLE OF HIGHER EDUCATION
Comparative Perspectives
edited by Ken Kempner
and William Tierney

DIMENSIONS OF THE COMMUNITY COLLEGE
International, Intercultural, and Multicultural Perspectives
edited by Rosalind Latiner Raby
and Norma Tarrow

THE LIBERAL ARTS COLLEGE ADAPTING TO CHANGE
The Survival of Small Schools
by Gary Bonvillian
and Robert Murphy

REFORM AND CHANGE IN HIGHER EDUCATION
International Perspectives
edited by James E. Mauch and
Paula L.W. Sabloff

SCIENCE AND TECHNOLOGY IN CENTRAL AND EASTERN EUROPE
The Reform of Higher Education
edited by A.D. Tillett
and Barry Lesser

CHINA'S UNIVERSITIES, 1895–1995
A Century of Cultural Conflict
by Ruth Hayhoe

THE FUNDING OF HIGHER EDUCATION
International Perspectives
edited by Philip G. Altbach and
D. Bruce Johnstone

JESUIT EDUCATION AND SOCIAL CHANGE IN EL SALVADOR
by Charles J. Beirne

HIGHER EDUCATION IN CRISIS
New York in National Perspective
edited by William C. Barba

The Liberal Arts College Adapting to Change
The Survival of Small Schools

Gary Bonvillian
Robert Murphy

Garland Publishing, Inc.
New York and London
1996

Library of Congress Cataloging-in-Publication Data

Bonvillian, Gary.
    The liberal arts college adapting to change : the survival of small
schools / Gary Bonvillian and Robert Murphy.
        p.   cm. — (Garland reference library of social science ; vol. 1011.
Garland studies in higher education ; v. 9)
    Includes bibliographical references (p.   ) and index.
    ISBN 0-8153-1946-0 (alk. paper)
        1. Small colleges—United States—Case studies.   2. Education, Humanis-
tic—United States—Case studies.   3. Keuka College.   I. Murphy, Robert
(Robert M.)   II. Title.   III. Series: Garland reference library of social
science ; v. 1011.   IV. Series: Garland reference library of social
science. Garland studies in higher education ; vol. 9.
LB2328.32.U6B66   1996
378.1'542'0973—dc20   95-45053
                                                                   CIP

Printed on acid-free, 250-year-life paper
Manufactured in the United States of America

To Mary, Kathy, and our families
for their love and support
throughout this project.

Contents

Chapter V

Chapter VI

Series Editor's Preface

Higher education is a multifaceted phenomenon in modern society, combining a variety of institutions and an increasing diversity of students, a range of purposes and functions, and different orientations. The series combines research-based monographs, analyses, and discussions of broader issues and reference books related to all aspects of higher education. It is concerned with policy as well as practice from a global perspective. The series is dedicated to illuminating the reality of higher and postsecondary education in contemporary society.

Philip G. Altbach
Boston College

The Liberal Arts College Adapting to Change

CHAPTER I
INTRODUCTION

Purpose of the Book

This book presents the story of small schools in American higher education. Although its focus is on small liberal arts colleges, the general concepts in the various subject areas of organization, administration, and management of higher education are applicable to all institutions. This book is also about change and how colleges must adapt to the economic realities of managing complex organizations. In addition to administrators, boards, faculty, historians, and scholars of higher education will also find the book useful in understanding the challenges and opportunities facing small schools.

The book will provide a brief historical perspective of small, liberal arts colleges and, perhaps, even a glimpse into their future. These unique institutions tell a compelling story as they have continuously evolved and met the challenge of change in this country's system of higher education. Their need to change has been driven by the financial and market forces which challenge academic leadership from all sectors of higher education to do more with less in an increasingly competitive climate for new students. Further, these changes are affecting the role of leadership and faculty and even the relationship an institution has with its many other constituencies such as students, parents, alumni, and employers. Finally, this book will tell the story of the small school's ability to adapt to change and survive as a distinctive component of our higher education system for nearly three hundred years in spite of the tenuous conditions under which many have operated.

Like most sectors of higher education, small schools are experiencing a transformation in how they function internally to meet the demands of external social and economic conditions. This transformation has also been influenced by the gradual introduction and development of new management practices in higher education, designed to strengthen the institution's position in the marketplace, while still maintaining their rich and useful traditions and heritage. Many academic leaders recognize the unique nature of the educational enterprise yet acknowledge that colleges have and will continue to be pressured to function with diminishing resources, making this transformation an imperative.

For several decades, we have witnessed colleges and universities attempt to gradually adopt traditional business practices in their drive to become more efficient, fiscally sound and competitive. This has resulted in many, still largely unanswered, questions with respect to optimal models for organizational design, institutional decision-making and strategic positioning. Each of these raises serious questions with respect to the changing role of administrators, faculty, and other major stakeholders who have a vested interest in the welfare of the institution. Thus, an analysis of the constraints and opportunities for these various groups, resulting from the many strategic issues confronting their institutions, will constitute a central theme of this book.

Relevance and Importance of the Topic

To assure the continued survival of small schools, leaders must be prepared to accept the fact that proven managerial techniques and practices can and are being applied to academic organizations. In recent years, consortium support groups such as The Council of Independent Colleges (CIC) as well as respected scholars in the management of higher education have called upon small schools to reconsider their traditional administrative and institutional decision-making practices and examine new approaches to managing the enterprise. Some schools have done so with considerable success. Several of their stories will be presented later in this book.

Of greater concern to those committed to new management and administrative practices is that traditional pathways to the formulation and execution of institutional decisions have relatively well-defined norms and patterns in higher education, ingrained over a long period of time and widely accepted in the academic community. Perhaps nowhere in higher education is this adherence to tradition stronger than in the small liberal arts school. As administration of these schools has become more complex and their vitality is increasingly dependent upon the application of sound management practices, such traditions are being threatened.

Faculty involvement and influence in institutional decision-making is often at the center of these discussions, as their historically held role in campus governance has resulted in a high expectation for continued participation. Today's academic leadership is challenged to meet these expectations while also assuring their institutions are strategically positioned in the marketplace. Striking a balance between these two demands is often a difficult one for college leadership. The challenge becomes exacerbated by the faculty's tendency to shy away from scrutiny of their own operating practices.

We often think of the strategic positioning of an institution as the prerogative of central administration. However, one emerging question, for all schools, is to what degree faculty should participate in this process. Prevailing questions in the study of institutional management and decision-making as well as campus governance are becoming less focused on which group should exert the most influence. Rather, we are beginning to see a greater interest in partnerships in decision-making, thus acknowledging the legitimate interest of all stakeholders and perhaps more importantly, capitalizing on the distinctive contributions each can make.

There is also a growing awareness and acceptance that the internal functions of the college will be influenced by external factors. Colleges must understand, be capable of adapting to and even learn to benefit from the changing environmental conditions which affect an institution's long-term vitality. Simply put, they can no longer afford to be static in an atmosphere of rapid change. Many small schools have demonstrated an ability to not only cope with but to even capitalize on these conditions, presenting evidence of their tenacity and will to survive.

Advocate organizations such as the Council of Independent Colleges (CIC) diligently work to both defend and promote the existence of small schools. Their portrayal of these institutions as vital national assets, should not be dismissed as merely promotional rhetoric. CIC offers the following points as an argument for both the success and long-term survival of small schools. Perhaps more importantly, it also provides us with a clearer understanding of the character of these unique organizations and reasons why we should seek to assure their existence.

- They each possess a distinctive institutional purpose. Intangible as it may be, these colleges are permeated with a special sense of purpose made up of an intrinsic mixture of historic ideals, moral and spiritual values, devotion to quality, and a clear and direct vision of the future--all with the individual student as the centerpiece.
- They emphasize teaching excellence. Professors teach students in personal settings--and not always in the formal classroom. Faculty research and publications are adjuncts to the teaching process.
- They provide education with a moral and spiritual dimension. Most small colleges were started by religious bodies. This religious heritage, while seldom proselytized, permeates the values of these colleges. They educate the whole person. The small size and residential nature of the colleges enable intimate personal contact among students, faculty, and administrators. Small colleges foster emotional, social, moral, and spiritual development of students--as well as intellectual growth. They emphasize the liberal arts and sciences.
- Because small colleges adhere to the values of

a liberal education, students find it impossible to overspecialize or to merely immerse themselves in vocational subjects. They are free and flexible. Beholden to no one but their own boards of trustees, small colleges march to the tune of their own drummer, not to the beat of a state planning bureau or a federal granting agency.

- They serve their region. Small colleges are sources of great local and regional pride. These colleges exist, in most cases, to serve the citizens of a particular region, even though they are privately supported and attract students from across the country. They are successful. In many cases for more than 200 years and in some cases for less than 20 years, small colleges have produced graduates who have succeeded, pioneered new programs, been the first, the best, the only in a field of endeavor.[1]

Among their other unique characteristics, small schools were, and perhaps still are today, the bastions of liberal arts. They relentlessly cling to the ideology of a liberal education. Even during the Progressive Era when colleges were under enormous pressure to respond with greater social service, they clung to a fundamental belief in a broad-based education. The small liberal arts colleges did respond but not at the expense of their commitment to their own educational philosophy. It was then, and still is today, one of their unique strategic strengths.

Rooted in the British tradition of teaching excellence and a core curriculum in the liberal arts, many colleges have evolved into multipurpose institutions providing a valuable service to society. While striving to maintain a unique identity among institutions of higher education, such as a fundamental commitment to undergraduate studies and their residential and even communal environment, liberal arts colleges also have survived by being responsive to a changing social climate.

In recent years, there has been relatively little published academic research and even less written in the popular literature on the history, evolution, and survival of small private liberal arts colleges. Yet, as will be illustrated, these unique organizations constitute a significant component of the higher education system.

In the early 1970s, several books were published which are frequently consulted by researchers in higher education. Alexander Astin and Calvin Lee authored one such book, *The Invisible Colleges* (McGraw-Hill, 1972) which addresses the impending challenges of small schools during a difficult economic period.[2] Labeled *invisible* by Astin and Lee due to the relative obscurity of the small schools, the term is also reflective of our general lack of understanding of this sector of higher education. In addition to this work, Burton Clark's *The Distinctive College* (originally published in 1970 by Aldine) was reissued in 1992 by Transaction Publishers.[3] This seminal work provides a clearer understanding of how the history, traditions, and values of an institution can greatly influence its character and survival.

In the 1980s, colleges and universities were also beginning to more closely examine the possible application of business principles such as strategic decision-making and marketing to their organizations. George Keller authored a popular book in 1983 on the application of strategic principles in higher education. Keller's *Academic Strategy, The Management Revolution in American Higher Education* (The Johns Hopkins University Press, 1983), presented a functional and easily interpreted model for examining the positioning of academic organizations.[4] Similarly, Philip Kotler and Karen Fox in their *Strategic Marketing for Educational Institutions* (Prentice Hall, 1985) illustrated that colleges and universities could adapt proven business principles to attract new students.[5]

While the Keller and Kotler/Fox books were instrumental in establishing a new interest in the management practices of higher education, they did not focus on the unique organizational conditions of small schools. Important contributions during their time and a basis for some of the work in this book, these publications did provide a new generation of institutional leadership with valuable insight into how traditional business principles and practices could be applied to academia.

Strategic Strengths and Market Realities

The small schools' historical commitment to the liberal arts and their apparent unity of purpose may yet prove to be the most significant strategic strength of these institutions. For some, however, it could also be their downfall. While their ideological roots provide a much-needed anchor for these institutions, like virtually all other colleges and universities, they have also become increasingly influenced by external social and economic conditions. External environmental conditions invariably affect the market and thus the appeal of any given institution to prospective students.

In recent years, this phenomenon has had a profound impact on traditional thinking within academia with respect to organizational structure, leadership, governance, and higher education's romantic emphasis on the campus as a community. As can be seen on virtually every campus today, regardless of size or character, a great many management decisions are being made to position the school for long-term competitiveness in the marketplace. Whether it is yet widely recognized or not, these are strategic decisions based on an analysis of the particular strengths of the institution as well as its ability to be responsive under continuously changing conditions.

On at least one front, the small school may have an inherent advantage in the strategic decision-making process which capitalizes on its primary resource, faculty. Recent research has shown the high degree to which faculty at private, four-year colleges are committed to students, their colleagues and the campus as a total community. In a study of faculty attitudes conducted by the University of California at Los Angeles Higher Education Research Institute, scores of different characteristics were measured in both public and private universities, four-year and two-year colleges. A number of characteristics of faculty from private four-year colleges emerged as evidence of their inherent commitment to the organization. They included:

- On the question of professional goals, in particular that of being a good colleague, these faculty ranked second (83.4%) within the six organizational types. Only public two-year colleges had a higher-ranked response.

- On the question of aspects of their jobs which they found to be very satisfactory or satisfactory as related to relationships with their fellow faculty, they again ranked second (79.7%) to public two-year colleges.
- On the question of the faculty's commitment to the welfare of the institution, they ranked first (87.1%) and significantly higher than in any other categories.
- On the question of whether administrators consider faculty concerns when making policy, these faculty ranked first (61.5%) and significantly higher than most other organizational types.
- On the question of importance of developing a sense of community among students and faculty, these faculty ranked first (60.6%) and significantly higher than all other categories.[6]

As will be reinforced throughout this book, it is imperative that today's leaders in small schools not only recognize but also utilize this high level of commitment of faculty while managing their organizations. While colleges and universities in the United States are preparing to meet mounting challenges of the late 1990s and beyond, this period could be a major turning point for higher education. While some institutions have historically survived and even thrived under such conditions, academic leaders today are less certain their institutions can weather such a challenging period without a close examination of the organization's strategic direction and optimization of all resources.

In spite of their vulnerabilities, most of the small private liberal arts colleges in the United States survived the turbulent decade of the 1980s. Innovative strategic initiatives were undertaken in response to the shifting demographics and an increasingly competitive market for new students. Today's enlightened academic leaders recognize that long-term institutional survival, assured by sound strategic decision-making, is a process best achieved through the collective efforts of both administration and other major stakeholders.

Institutional Realities

On the brink of permanently closing the institution in 1983, Keuka College, in upstate New York, is a shining example of the strength and resiliency of these small schools and their potential to execute strategic decisions. Keuka College, to be profiled later in this book, is an example of one institution which defied the odds and successfully recovered from near collapse in the early 1980s.

Led by an aggressive new president, over the past ten years Keuka has reached the highest student enrollment in the institution's one-hundred year history and completed its most successful capital campaign. Given his reputation and record of achievement, it was tempting to simply look at Keuka's success as the accomplishment of the current president, Arthur Kirk. Kirk, like most presidents, was certainly a key player in the turnaround of Keuka. However, this is not a story of a white knight. Keuka's success is also due to the dedication, talent, and willingness of many others in the organization to meet the challenge.

As is true of hundreds of other small schools across the country, Keuka's story is one of a community bonded together by a sense of purpose and a shared vision for the liberal arts. It is a story of people, from the tough and sometimes single-minded administrative leadership core to the restless but committed faculty and tireless staff. It is also a story of students, many of whom, it would appear, still come to Keuka for the same reasons that they have throughout its long history. Keuka's story is also an example of the emotional swings which can sweep a campus when struggling to survive. Finally, it is a story of the challenges which every campus faces in the United States today, but perhaps more profoundly in this sector.

Recovery from near collapse is a tumultuous process for any institution, and Keuka, like many other small schools over the past decade, struggled through its transformation and rebuilding. Several important organizational issues emerged throughout the rebuilding period which caused concern and even tension between administration and faculty. Of particular note was the impact that managing through a crisis would have on the historical and traditional patterns of decision-making in the institution.

Keuka's story, in particular, exemplified the magnitude of the challenge facing leadership in their introduction of new, and often radical, methodologies for managing the institution. The following points were captured in the close examination of Keuka's story and further evidenced in other small college cases examined for this book. They will be explored in greater detail throughout subsequent chapters:

- It is accepted that the majority of faculty and administration in small schools have a desire to preserve many of the characteristics which made them unique among other institutions of higher education, including a strong identity with the campus as an integrated community and a universal commitment to the long-term welfare and survival of the organization.
- While leaders of these schools acknowledge the need to engage the community in the process of strategic decision-making, they have not yet reconciled this objective with the tendency, and often times, necessity, to control decisions centrally.
- Faculty believe a once-strong voice in institutional decision-making has been lost due to the pressure to yield to market conditions and new administrative practices.

A Final Note

Attempts to rationalize the world around us and the self-serving tendencies which invariably afflict various stakeholders in an academic institution lead many to the conclusion that emotions and irrational behavior all too often dominate organizational decision-making. College and universities have been built on a Greek concept that such institutions should be a marketplace of ideas where the weight of logic, data, and documentation should carry the day.

Unfortunately, such ideals in managing colleges and universities often elude those who have most control over the enterprise. A high degree of rationality in decision-making is not inherently a characteristic of a dynamic environment such as a college or university. The inability of academic leaders to reconcile rational decision-making within a dynamic organization can result in cynicism and a genuine sense of despair among faculty as everyone strives for the ideal, yet decisions are sometimes made based on coalitions, cronyism, and good old-fashioned politics.

Baldridge, Curtis, Ecker, and Riley, in their study of academic governance, allude to the prevalence of the domineering political model in institutions of higher education.[7] While generally acknowledging the existence of collegiality in all institutions, the political model seems foremost in their consciousness as they explain how educational institutions operate. Further, the *Zeitgeist Effect* can amplify the impression that the political model is also quite often dominant, particularly during troubled times.

This reality of politicism in troubled colleges need not be a constraint if recognized and directly addressed by all those in a position to affect change. Not doing so jeopardizes a school's ability to make the necessary and timely decisions for survival in a competitive environment. Making necessary and timely decisions further presumes an adherence to order and even a systems perspective of managing an institution. While many of the models for decision-making presented in this book presume an institution's ability to develop such systems and maintain order in the process, the constraints and realities of academia's unique internal environment are recognized.

One of the themes of this book, and the new wave of thinking with respect to academic management and administration, is that all major institutional decision-making today must be viewed within the context of external and internal environments. While external environments create the impetus for change, only through internal reflection will any organization successfully react and meet the challenge.

Those closest to the small schools recognize there are many characteristics of these unique academic organizations which should not be compromised for the sake of short-term survival. In fact, to do so would be contrary to what has been beneficial in sustaining their existence to date. In spite of the prescriptive tone of the many messages of this book, in the end analysis, only the individual school can define the pathway for decision-making which best fits its needs and functions within the existing internal environment. Use what follows as a guide in analyzing your own unique organization.

CHAPTER II
THE LIBERAL ARTS COLLEGE

Historical Roots

European Influence

The small liberal arts college has been a distinctive component of the United States system of higher education for nearly three hundred years. Historians point to the late 1800s as the period of greatest proliferation for these schools, yet their beginnings can be traced back to Colonial America. Colonial settlers, largely influenced by their European heritage, recognized that colleges were necessary to assure future generations of well-educated civil and religious leaders.

While Harvard, William and Mary, Yale, and Dartmouth, the first institutions of higher education in the United States, and all founded before 1770, are not today considered small liberal arts colleges, it is from their roots that the entire system has evolved. From the standpoint of the curriculum, these early colleges were committed to an education that was "formed by the values, ideas, and practices of the Renaissance and Reformation...an education deemed proper for a gentlemen and...a knowledge of the classical literature as advocated by the humanists."[1] As such, the small liberal arts colleges were also destined to extend the values and culture of a European society, much of which America's early settlers had sought to leave behind in other ways of life.

While America's own social development over the ensuing two hundred years would gradually change the character of these schools, many aspects of this European heritage would remain, even into the modern era. Europe's rich history also served to provide stability for these fragile institutions throughout this nation's rapid and sometimes volatile periods of growth. These influences are still recognizable in today's colleges through their formal rituals and even organizational structure.

A sense of order and control was characteristic of how the early colleges viewed student life and, in the English tradition, these schools were meant to serve as an alternative for the homes young people left behind. There was an emphasis on teaching rather than study, on students rather than scholars, and on order and discipline, rather than learning.[2] This perspective of collegial life would continue to be an important element in the future character and appeal of the small liberal arts college. The paternal nature of these schools was, and still is today, an attractive feature for prospective students, but perhaps even more importantly for their parents. As will be discussed later, many believe this characteristic to be one of the most important and endearing in the competitive student market.

Evolution and Change

The character of these schools did take a noticeable turn following the Revolutionary War. As a result of the rapid push westward and expansion of commercial activities, many educators saw colleges as potential training grounds for a new breed of leaders to guide the development of a burgeoning nation. While still retaining a strong commitment to their religious and classical roots, a more practical and functional view of the role of colleges was developing.

The debates in higher education today over the degree to which a curriculum should be applied and practical can be traced to this early turn of events. Such debates were not limited to the United States' system. Although our vision of a curriculum model for the liberal arts was based on the traditions of Oxford and Cambridge, historians would also note that the European educational system was generally focused on professional education.

The applied perspective in the United States and abroad ultimately influenced the advancement of science as a staple of the curriculum, resulting in the beginning of colleges' transitions to their more modern and purposeful role in society. Attending college in the 1800s was certainly not seen as a means of advancing oneself socially, at least not to the degree that it is today. However, perhaps as a natural extension of America's love affair with personal success, colleges did begin to serve such a purpose. As America grew and prospered as a nation, so, too, did the social and economic demands of its people. Frederick Rudolph captures this change in his historical account of the transformation of colleges and universities in America:

> Inevitably the American college would face up to the self-made man on his own terms and in the process discover a new purpose (for colleges). In the end, it became necessary to argue and possible to prove, on the basis of selected individuals, that going to college was a way of making more money

than if you did not. In the very early years such an idea had not been an expressed purpose of the colleges. But the time came when graduates discovered that a college education as social investment was now of less importance than a college education as a personal investment.[3]
This sir, is my case. It is the case, not merely of that humble institution, it is the case of every college in the land. It is more. It is the case of every eleemosynary institution throughout the country...the case of every man who has property of which he may be stripped...for the question is simply this: Shall our state legislature be allowed to take that which is not their own, to turn it from its original use, and apply it to such ends or purposes as they, in their discretion shall see fit. Sir, you may destroy this little institution...,but if you do...you extinguish, one after another, all those great lights of science, which, for more than a century, have thrown their radiance over the land! It is sir, as I have said, a small college, and yet there are those that love it...[6]

Between 1850 and 1899, a total of 212 small liberal arts colleges were founded. According to Astin & Lee, the small liberal arts college sector was primarily shaped by three historical factors: (1) the religious influence in America before the Civil War, (2) educational expectations for emancipated slaves and, (3) an increasing demand for technical schools.[7]

Frederick Rudolph describes the proliferation of the small liberal arts college during the 1800s as a sign of the progressive, if not irrational, nature of our country's period of expansion.[8] Like the entrepreneurial spirit which was sweeping through American business and industry, the small liberal arts college was indeed in its boom years. Historians of higher education point to a number of reasons for this phenomenon including the most commonly held and accepted premise of denominational propagation. Church leaders in the nineteenth century recognized that United States expansionism was also fraught with temptation for the individual. Many opportunities and choices for young men, and women, would soon present themselves in commerce as well as education. From a more modern perspective, the founding of sectarian colleges could be viewed as a strategic decision to position the church's influence in a rapidly changing social order.

There were other important reasons for the expansion of small schools in American higher education. They were among the first to provide educational opportunities to the newly emancipated slaves. Even prior to the War, as many as six educational institutions were established for those slaves who were already freed. Because of the obvious social and educational disadvantages which beset this population following the Civil War, the focus of these schools was more on remediation and less on vocational and utilitarian studies and would not even be classified as colleges, by today's standards.[9]

The small liberal arts college did become the developmental ground for coeducation in the United States, with Oberlin enrolling four women in 1837. However, prior to the Civil War, fewer than a dozen colleges adopted coeducation.[10] As a result, these colleges struggled, from their very beginnings, with a variety of gender-related issues including sexism in the curriculum, classroom, and campus community. These pioneers in coeducation were among the first institutions of society to acknowledge that both men and women would eventually share in the challenges as well as opportunities of social responsibility.

Throughout much of the 1800s many schools which were still holding to their all-male traditions suffered and even collapsed. At least in part, the small schools' willingness to embrace an egalitarian perspective of education was driven by the need to compete with an emerging university system. University enrollment by the late 1800s shifted so dramatically in favor of women, relative to small liberal arts colleges, there was a perceived imbalance in some institutions. In 1870 there was one woman student to 429 men in universities; in 1898 these figures had become 588 women and 745 men. This tremendous increase in enrollment of women at larger universities such as Northeastern caused such a concern, that engineering was added to the curriculum just to counter the perceived imbalance.[11]

Since technical schools, at that time, were clearly designed for a predominantly male enrollment, this curricular device to control sex ratios also served to create a distinction between the still-held beliefs regarding masculine versus feminine subject matter. This distinction has greatly influenced the evolving character of the small liberal arts colleges which, over time, and until at least recently, predominantly leaned towards the liberal arts and, thus, historically enrolled more women.

Lawrence Veysey refers to one of several educational perspectives which emerged following the Civil War as the *liberal culture*, which is characterized as resisting the practical or utilitarian forms of study found in colleges and universities...also, more commonly referred to as a liberal education.[12]

R.E. Jones, President of Hobart, expanding on this theme, said that the aim of the colleges was "social common sense," and they should promote "conformity with reality, social sanity, and fitness for practical life." They should do this by "aiming to stimulate general culture and to train character...by furnishing sound and successful training in the laws and arts of life [and] by ridding pupils of their boyish irresponsibility."[13]

Due to a heightened social reform movement, higher education was under increasing pressure to contribute to the betterment of society. Public service and a sense of responsibility were to create a better America.

The Modern Era of Small Colleges

Growth and Prosperity

If the Industrial Revolution was the fuel for educational reform, World War I was the flame which ignited schools of all types to meet the challenge of a powerful nation. The War became a catalyst for reform as society began to accept an obligation to extend and perpetuate the ideals of this country. At the forefront of this reform was an acceptance of business as a legitimate area of study and the preparation of professional managers as a necessity. The alignment of higher education and the business elite at the turn of the century was no accident. Notables such as

Andrew Carnegie, Cornelius Vanderbilt, Leland Stanford, and John D. Rockefeller began to recognize education as an investment in the future of American enterprise.[14]

The small liberal arts schools responded accordingly, and many began introducing business courses into their curriculum. Antioch College not only transformed itself into one of the most respected small schools in the nation but also introduced a new idea for cooperative relations with business and industry. Antioch's work-study curriculum, adapted in 1920, resulted in the schools growing from 75 students to over 700 by 1926.[15] It was an idea which appealed to both businessmen as well as prospective students who saw their future in the commercial sector.

In spite of the reform pressures, President Jones' statement is still an accurate reflection of the balance we might expect to find between the liberal and professional programs in small colleges throughout the country. In this sense, small schools have created yet another niche in the market for undergraduate students. By remaining committed to their founding missions of a broad-based education yet exhibiting an ability to meet the challenges of change, small colleges have continued to play an important role in undergraduate education.

For much of the first half of this century, all of higher education enjoyed unprecedented growth. Both the small college and the university sector benefitted from society's acknowledgement that higher education led to prosperity for the individual as well as the nation. Three primary factors attributed to this growth: (1) a public commitment, supported financially, to expand access to higher education; (2) a belief that the nation's welfare was dependent on an educated populace; and (3) an increase in the utilization of colleges and universities to advance the agricultural, industrial, and cultural needs of society.[16]

Also during this time period, the educational system itself was expanding, to include a new concept for two-year colleges. It was an idea which some believe posed a potential threat to the less selective small liberal arts schools. In time, this new type of institution would position itself among the other four-year colleges and universities and establish its own unique role in the United States' system of higher education.

Enrollment patterns throughout the following decades for all sectors reflect a steady growth. From the financial perspective, many schools were also beginning to establish a stronger fiscal base on which to build for the future. The period from the 1940s through the 1960s are sometimes referred to as the Golden Years of higher education as several social and economic factors greatly influenced a student's willingness and ability to attend college.[17] Not only was attending college seen as the definitive path for success, the public was also willing to provide the needed support to further encourage access, thus attracting an increasingly diverse student body.

A series of legislative acts, following World War II, solidified the government's role in substantially subsidizing a college education. The GI Bill of 1944 provided opportunity in colleges and universities for 2.3 million veterans and was a major factor in further expanding mass access to higher education.[18] This act was followed by the National Defense Education Act of 1958, which provided students with a low-interest student loan program and the

Higher Education Act of 1965 (amended in 1972), which offered students at private colleges a selection of federal grant and loan and work-study programs which were specifically designed to assist students from low to middle-income families.[19]

Crisis in Higher Education

For all of higher education, but perhaps more profoundly in the small school sector, the fortunes of the previous period began to erode around 1970 as enrollments began to peak, inflation swept the nation, and a general overextension of all campus resources from the past several decades left many schools vulnerable. Unfortunately, most schools were not prepared for such a dramatic turn of events. This sense of immunity from the social and economic environmental factors fostered by unfettered growth not only caused a great uncertainty for the future of many schools, it also gave rise to a new interest in better understanding the complex nature of managing colleges and universities.

By the early 1970s the challenges facing small liberal arts colleges were becoming apparent to the academy.

- The value of their curricula was being called into question by the trend towards vocationalism.
- These schools were more severely affected by the cost-income squeeze than were most other categories of institutions. They were generally small and without any substantial economies of scale, and even a slight decrease in enrollment

moved them back up a steep cost curve that reflected high fixed overhead costs.

- They were generally unitary institutions, and it was hard to lop off any sizable endeavors in order to cut costs.
- Because of their location and fierce sense of independence, movements to merge or to form consortia of these institutions have produced few major changes.
- Since they relied most heavily on tuition, they were very vulnerable to competition from public institutions.
- Their search for new vocational programs to supplement teacher education might have attracted students but raised fears that they were compounding their problems by diluting their main strengths.[20]

Current Challenges

Surviving Difficult Times

We often refer to higher education in the United States today as a system. This system is represented by a variety of alternative types of colleges and universities that provide a diversity of opportunities and experiences. Small liberal arts colleges represent a large segment of this system and can be characterized as encompassing the full range of selectivity, quality, and religious beliefs of our society.

Depending on how one elects to categorize the schools by factors such as size, selectivity, and reputation, these schools represent approximately 750 of the 3,500 institutions in the United States.[21] This system was recently refined when the Carnegie Foundation established a new classification scheme which more accurately reflects the changes in programmatic offerings in these institutions.

The 1987 revision to the classifications categorized liberal arts colleges into two groups. Group I colleges had selective admissions and awarded at least half of their baccalaureate degrees in liberal arts. Group II colleges were less selective and awarded at least half of their baccalaureate degrees in liberal arts. To account for the changing character of these institutions, approximately 70 percent of the Group II schools were reclassified, indicating that a majority of their programs were in professional areas.

The new system, presented in the April 6, 1994 edition of *The Chronicle of Higher Education*, classifies both groups as Baccalaureate (Liberal Arts) I or II. Group I is still the selective category, but these colleges need only have 40 percent of their baccalaureate degrees in the liberal arts. Group II is still less selective and generally has fewer than 40 percent of their degrees in the liberal arts.[22] This revision is reflective of the natural evolution the liberal arts schools have been experiencing for the better part of this century in their movement towards a more comprehensive offering of programs and meeting the changing needs of society.

One of the most frequently cited works on the condition of small private colleges by Alexander W. Astin and Calvin B.T. Lee poignantly reminds us of the threat which these schools constantly face:

From time to time, it is suggested that most of these *invisible* colleges should be allowed to decline and eventually die out. Usually, the arguments behind this suggestion are that the invisible colleges are of poor quality; that they no longer serve a real mission; that they do not attract enough students to warrant their continued existence; that they duplicate the resources and functions of other higher education institutions; and that they are too inefficient and too wasteful to justify any attempt to keep afloat.[23]

Interestingly, the bleak picture portrayed in literature from the early 1970s on the small liberal arts colleges has yielded to a more optimistic and visionary perspective of their role and future in society. The social and economic conditions of the country over the past twenty years and the fact that many of these schools have simply survived in spite of the predictions in all probability have something to do with this phenomenon.

Although many variables have affected the continued existence of the majority of these small schools over the past twenty years, three major themes will be highlighted. The themes appear consistently throughout the literature as primary challenges to the survival of these institutions into the twenty-first century.

Preservation of Their Unique Character

First is the question of size. E.F. Schumacher (1973) authored a provocative book on the virtues of smallness that, although not specifically directed at education, proved to be a consciousness-raising piece on economies of scale. Schumacher's message was that, as a society, we must be prepared to deal with a multiplicity of small-scale units, as they constitute the integral components or, as he states, "the articulated structure" of our existence. His emphasis is on people, not just science and technology, which has tended to dominate our thinking over much of this century.[24]

Interestingly, the downsizing of work units, marginally popularized by Schumacher's work in the early 1970s, is experiencing a revival. This phenomenon is a result of a variety of factors influencing the competitive positioning of American business and industry and an organization's ability to motivate its workforce to increase productivity while also being constrained by diminishing resources.

Critics of the small liberal arts college have suggested that to be effective and efficient, a school needs an enrollment of between 1,500 and 2,000 students.[25] The Council of Independent Colleges (CIC), an advocacy organization which supports the initiatives of small private institutions throughout the United States, vigorously defends the virtues of being small and counters its critics with the following facts:

A common myth suggests that small colleges--supposedly lacking economies of scale--are by definition less efficient than larger institutions. This is false. In a detailed economic analysis of institutions enrolling fewer than 1000 students, an American Council on Education study failed to find data to support this conclusion: "The decision of the most appropriate size for a liberal arts college should not be made on economic or financial grounds."[26]

Dr. Arthur Kirk, president of Keuka College, said that the small school may actually have a strategic advantage in the competitive market for students.[27] His position is based on the small school's ability to be more responsive to the changing conditions in which all institutions must compete. Indeed, as shall be seen in this book and throughout much of the literature which addresses the strategic process, leadership is one of the most important variables discussed. The influence of a single individual, such as the president of a small institution, can be profound. CIC provides the following as a convincing argument for this claim:

Small colleges, unencumbered by bureaucracy and having fewer administrative obstacles, can readily adapt to change. People can exchange information quickly and decisions can be made swiftly. Innovations can be implemented rapidly. In this environment, a single individual--an imaginative president, for example, can wield significant influence over an institution. It is far more difficult to alter the course of larger institutions. Presidents of small colleges are like sailors of a single ship, tacking this way and that, catching the winds of opportunity, trying to round the buoy first--and safely. At small institutions, leadership has a real chance to function.[28]

Over the past decade, business and industry have discovered the virtues of downsizing, and many companies have embraced the ideology of smaller work units. Management gurus from the 1980s such as Tom Peters have perpetuated Schumacher's theories, saying, "The economic theorists may disagree, but to the excellent company, the evidence is crystal clear--smallness is both effective and efficient. Smallness induces manageability and above all, commitment. Small works. Small is beautiful."[29]

History, tradition, values, and the ideology of community are elements which contribute to the institutional cohesiveness of the small liberal arts college. These elements of organizational character provide a common sense of purpose for the college as a total community and often serve to hold people together through the most difficult of times. Over time, they also become ingrained in the life and continued existence of the organization. Taken to its extreme, some schools develop such a strong commitment to their own purpose and existence, their cultural perspective assumes an even stronger role in the long-term viablility of the institution. Burton Clark's study and characterization of Antioch, Reed, and Swarthmore as extreme examples of institutional saga is a reflection of the level of intensity this idea of organizational culture can reach.[30]

Not all small liberal arts colleges could claim to possess the richness of culture or saga as would be found in an Antioch, Reed, or Swarthmore. However, as Clark was attempting to portray in his study of these unique institutions, many small liberal arts colleges develop similar patterns of intense identification with their communities, curriculum, faculty, and, of course, students. Central to the development of an organizational culture is the role of faculty. Faculty carry a large responsibility in both nurturing and perpetuating the unique characteristics of the small liberal arts college. Their focus on students and teaching may contribute more to the ideology of community than any other activity on campus. In a study conducted by the Carnegie Foundation for the Advancement of Teaching, students consistently rated faculty in small liberal arts colleges higher than in other institutional types on the following points:

- Overall, I am satisfied with the teaching I have received. Professors at my college take a personal interest in my academic progress.
- Professors encourage students to discuss their feelings about important issues.
- On the whole, I trust the faculty here to look out for students' interest.
- There are professors at my college whom I feel free to turn to for advice on personal matters.
- Professors encourage students to participate in classroom discussion.[31]

The conditions under which the faculty/student relationship has an opportunity to grow and develop is essential to the general welfare of the school. Consistently, it is found that students select and attend these schools and faculty carry out their careers for the very reasons cited above. The challenge for these small schools is to not compromise the unique characteristics which built their reputations and resulted in a true niche in the educational market.

Implications of Yielding to Market Pressures

Shifting demographics and, specifically, a reduction in the availability of traditional college-age students, rocketing costs of higher education, increasing competition from the public sector schools and declining financial support from government are the reasons most often cited for why the small liberal arts colleges may not survive. Inherent in this presumption is that they are not capable of responding to changing external conditions. Historians would disagree with this position and point to the past two hundred years as evidence that:

> although the major objectives of the private liberal arts college have been leadership training, general preparation for vocational eminence, character development and the transmission of cultural heritage...periodic shifts of emphasis among these continuing and closely related objectives delineate the history of American collegiate development...first one and then another justification became predominant as the liberal arts college sought to make itself relevant to a constantly changing society.[32]

Perhaps we should be asking ourselves not whether these schools will survive but how and what is the implication for higher education in the United States as a total system. Others have already begun to ask these relevant questions in the continuing studies on the survival of small schools:

- Will liberal arts colleges, in the face of demands for more career-oriented undergraduate majors, forsake their traditional commitment to liberal education for a panoply of vocational majors?
- Will private institutions begin to lose their distinctiveness with the higher education community?
- Can the liberal arts college interpret itself to a diversity of publics, including potential students as well as the American business and professional communities, in such a way as to make clear the personal and social benefits of a liberal education?[33]

The question of forsaking their liberal arts roots is not insignificant for these small schools, and the literature suggests that it is a serious one as they shape their future. The recent reclassification of small schools, as previously mentioned, indicates that, for many, it may no longer be appropriate to consider them as liberal arts institutions. Rather, they have become small professional colleges. Such reclassification can have an impact on both student and faculty recruiting and the costs of operations.

In spite of the pressure to specialize, most of these schools fiercely cling to this liberal arts tradition. In fact, not to do so may put them at a far greater risk in the marketplace, as it is unlikely they could compete directly with the larger, more specialized institutions. Critics of the tendency of some small schools to become miniversities caution that such initiatives could jeopardize the intimacy and sense of community which are the cornerstones of these unique institutions.[34]

By clinging to their historic core mission in the liberal arts, they actually maintain a niche in the market no other group of schools can legitimately claim. While attracting new enrollment is quite often the number one priority of these schools, their ability to provide educational opportunity to the broadest spectrum of the population may also prove to be an advantage in the marketplace. It is also important to remember that the tradition of the liberal arts college, two hundred years old before the birth of the American university, in effect, dictated that the university would have an undergraduate level of somewhat general or liberal education.[35]

Relative to the public sector schools, state support for private institutions has never been of great significance. However, federal and state financial aid programs for disadvantaged students are particularly attractive to the small, private, and generally less selective school. Proponents of these small schools suggest that (1) at the federal level, small private liberal arts colleges are likely to benefit more from the expansion of student-aid programs than from any other government policy and (2) at the state level, development of student-aid programs, especially those that accommodate a somewhat high tuition level and those having eligibility criteria accommodating middle-income students, will also benefit small liberal arts colleges.[36] Eligibility based solely on need, not academic achievement, will benefit institutions that are less selective than more prestigious institutions.

Of particular concern to many of these schools is the

enticement and temptation which this type of public policy can present to a struggling institution. Already criticized for their relaxed admissions standards, few can claim membership to the club of elite schools which enjoy exemplary reputations and can draw students nationally. This occasionally results in a crisis of identity among their peer group. While they have been criticized for their lack of selectivity in admissions, the small liberal arts colleges claim to be serving a wider range of students in society. Given the nature of federal-and state-supported financial aid packages, this has often been to their advantage. With trends towards cutting publicly supported assistance, it can also be a problem for these tuition-driven institutions. It is a two-edged sword.

Ironically, this market opportunity also presents a dilemma for the small private school as the value of independence is now compromised by the encroachment of increased government influence. CIC proudly proclaims that their institutions are:

> Beholden to no one but their own Boards of Trustees; independent colleges march to the tune of their own drummer, not to the beat of state planning agencies or the federal government. Their small size and private ownership means they can add programs, change policies, and implement innovative ideas at will--qualities critical in a changing world.[37]

In reality, only a very few institutions could make such a bold claim. Public funds influence the behavior of many colleges and universities. The question for these small independent schools is the degree to which they will ultimately compromise their values, traditions, and commitment to the liberal arts.

Clark Kerr cautioned such compromise and warns, "The curriculum should be more than just the sum of the consequences of internal and external pressures."[38] As an undergraduate at Swarthmore and, later, as a teacher at Antioch, Kerr recognized early in his distinguished career the value of the liberal arts mission. He places the responsibility for maintaining the integrity of the liberal arts and its important role in society squarely on the college president. We will examine this responsibility as well as that of all the major stakeholders of these insitutions in later chapters.

In Summary

These first two chapters have provided the foundation for a better understanding of the origins and evolution of small schools in this country. Such a perspective is critical to further understand and appreciate their contributions to our higher education system and their truly unique characteristics. Their propensity for survival and historical ability to adapt, in spite of the economic and market challenges, should indicate to their critics that they represent a significant force in higher education.

We can now turn our attention to what many have accomplished and are prepared to show others in their efforts to better manage and strategically position themselves in the marketplace. The following chapters will profile Keuka College and a number of schools and specific initiatives which are considered essential among those who have embraced new practices of institutional decision-making.

CHAPTER III
A CASE STUDY OF
KEUKA COLLEGE

Many of the traditions, values, and pride of distinction in the small-school sector are rooted in the work and vision of the founding fathers who created an ideological foundation still visible in the programs, people, and campus communities today. It is at the center of what many schools believe they are and have to offer in this competitive arena of higher education. The ideology of these small schools holds together even through difficult times.

The following two chapters are excerpts from a case study which attempted to better understand how one small school has not only survived but even thrived under adverse conditions, carrying forth the vision of its founding fathers for over one hundred years. The case is a result of over two years of an in-depth and on-site study of one school's history, organizational changes, leadership, and role of stakeholders in institutional decisions. The resulting report would not have been possible without the full cooperation of the Keuka community. Over fifty confidential interviews were conducted with faculty, staff, alumni, students, and administration. In addition, access to archival documents provided a picture into Keuka's past. Finally, the work of historian Philip Africa and his book, *Keuka College: A History* (Judson, 1974), contributed a great deal to the retrospective of this small school's early years.[1]

Keuka College is an example of what the small school is capable of achieving in spite of the odds. Keuka's situation also illustrates how an institution's history, traditions, and values can be linked to a modern perspective of strategic management.

Evolution of a College Community

Keuka College: 1890-1916

The Free Baptists

Founded in 1890, Keuka College in upstate New York possesses many of the same organizational characteristics which can be found in hundreds of small schools which dot the United States. Like hundreds of other institutions founded in the late 1800s by denominational interest groups, Keuka has strong religious roots. Believing in the tenet that man was free to mark out his own course--and a free moral agent, the Free Baptist Church founded many institutions throughout the United States, including Keuka College. Although they did not intend to interfere with local autonomy of any institution, the Free Baptists did form a Central Association to coordinate and pool the resources of their churches in New York and Pennsylvania. It was by this Association and the driving force of one man in particular, Dr. George H. Ball, a Baptist minister, that Keuka was established.

Although Keuka distinguished itself throughout most of the twentieth century as a woman's college, many people are not aware that it actually began as a coeducational institution. Keuka's first president, Dr. Ball, envisioned a people's college--where the children of the region would be educated. In 1890, 134 young men and women, coming largely from homes within a one-day trip of the campus, arrived as the charter class of Keuka Institute.

Keuka received a provisional charter from the State of New York in 1892. In this provision, Keuka was required to secure $100,000, invested as endowment or remunerative property, before conferring any actual degrees. In 1896, Keuka met this requirement, and three students entered degree programs which included courses in Latin, Greek, mathematics, English, history, science, philosophy, and drawing. Keuka's first two college graduates completed their requirements in 1900.

Keuka Park

Student experiences at Keuka were not limited to the classroom. Dr. Ball's plan was to build a community, not merely a campus. This community would be committed to the intellectual, spiritual, and cultural enrichment of all its residents. An undated and unsigned brochure from those early years describes Dr. Ball's vision:

A family of ideas led to this understanding. A vigorous academy; a thorough college; a great summer assembly; a college town, where families shall reside while their children are in school; positive religious surroundings without sectarian bias; plainness and cheapness of living; freedom from saloon temptations; delightful scenery; income from the college building, by using it for boarding purposes during summer vacations; attaching families to the school by the sale of lots on the Park to persons all over the land; thousands interested in the college by means of the summer assemblies in the immense grove, and the courses of lectures at these assemblies also attracting great attention; these are some of the ideas which are incorporated in the enterprise.[2]

There was virtually no separation of the college from the surrounding area which became known as Keuka Park. Through the initial purchase of a large parcel of land, known then as the Ketchum farm, the Central Association was able to sell off up to 775 lots to future Park residents. Initial sales were brisk, bringing in the required revenue to build Keuka's main building. Ball Hall, a magnificent structure which towers above all other buildings in the area, still stands today as a reminder of the optimism and vision of Keuka's founders.

Linkages with Business and Industry

One might be tempted to conclude that Keuka's communal nature would isolate it from a rapidly changing social and industrial order at the turn of the century. This was not the case, and, in fact, Keuka's leadership recognized the need to both educate as well as train young people for the world of work. Their early and continuing commitment to the liberal arts as a core curriculum complements an equal interest in preparing both men and women through programs which leadership described as training of which business men could approve.

Cooperative efforts with local business enterprises were not unusual for Keuka and probably were instrumental in the institution's historical belief in a practical education. One early venture was the establishment of the Keuka Park Sanitarium, later becoming an inn and ultimately a dormitory. There was also a joint venture with the nearby town of Penn Yan and the Pulteney Telephone Company as well as a farm, operational well into the twentieth century.

The business enterprise most frequently referred to in Keuka's early history was the development of a basket factory, a logical product given the growing number of vineyards in the surrounding county. Dr. Ball saw the Keuka Park Basket Company as both a means of generating revenue for the perennial challenges of budget as well as providing individual students a source of personal income and practical experience. Keuka was a pioneer in work-study and proudly promoted its opportunities for students to be part of modern manufacturing.

Closing the College

Between 1908 and 1915, Keuka floundered, mainly due to the combination of losing a principal benefactor in the Ball family as well as its drifting away from the Central Association of the Free Baptists. Keuka's financial base was never properly established beyond the good will of the Ball family and the Baptist Church. Even the business ventures which were designed to both generate revenue and provide a means for student work could not cover the mounting debts.

While the Free Baptists had hoped some of the commercial endeavors of Keuka College might offset expenditures, none was successful enough to meet this objective. There was also a modest effort to recruit more individuals to the board of trustees with the financial means to boost Keuka's private gift giving.

For over twenty-five years, Keuka had fought a valiant battle to establish a unique educational community in which the intellectual, social, spiritual and cultural needs of the individual were addressed. The final classes of the coeducational institution ended in June 1916, causing many of the remaining students to transfer to nearby Hobart College.

To the credit of the founding fathers, Keuka had been becoming recognized as a respected small liberal arts school in the east. When it ceased classes, the facilities had grown to include: Ball Hall, the Lucina, the old basket factory, Dr. Ball's Cottage residence, the Stanley House in which the very first classes were held, and the original barn of the Ketchum farm. An interview with a member of the Barrus family, conducted in 1958, revealed that even when the institution closed, Sunday Chapel was still held in Ball Hall in hopes that the College would eventually re-open.

Keuka College: 1917-1935

The Rebirth of Keuka

The sense of purpose and sheer tenacity which kept this small institution alive (even if only on the margin for the first twenty-five years) would also see it through the next fifty. The resurrection of Keuka as a college for women during this period is a story of both survival and courage to meet the challenges of a changing social order. Technically, Keuka never lost its official charter from the

State of New York. In 1920, the State declared Keuka's provisional charter that was established in 1892 was still active, and that the college had merely suspended instruction from 1916 until its re-opening in 1921. Those who had kept Keuka's hopes for survival alive seized the opportunity to reopen the institution.

Dr. Arthur H. Norton Builds a Community

As the first lay president of Keuka College for Women, Dr. Norton would be frequently quoted as saying that he had been "called to be the president of a college that had no faculty, no students and no charter, the three essentials of a college."[3] With respect to the charter, the State of New York did finally grant a permanent charter to Keuka in 1924.

For the times and the conditions under which Keuka would compete in the rapidly expanding market of colleges and universities, Arthur H. Norton was the consummate president. Throughout his sixteen years of dedicated service to Keuka, both the college and the greater community would expand and establish the foundation on which the institution would later thrive.

According to historical accounts, Dr. Norton borrowed against his life insurance to purchase three additional houses in Keuka Park, eventually to be used by faculty. This brought the total of houses available for incoming faculty to seven. His strong working relationship and credibility with faculty, most of whom he personally recruited, was exemplary. One member of the faculty described his relationship with the president in these terms:

every day we had a faculty meeting in the corner of the long room on the lake side second floor center of the building [Ball], used as the YMCA room during those first years. Those were memorable meetings. We began to discover how a great intellectual leader with a fine vision and an infinite amount of faith, courage, and humor thinks, and how simply and convincingly those thoughts can be expressed. I began to feel in those days--and the conviction grew--that we were going forward with an Abraham Lincoln spirit at the helm.[4]

In what today we might characterize as a sound strategic decision, Keuka was about to catch the wave of a burgeoning women's movement. Nineteen twenty-one was a good year to launch a women's college, and it was not difficult to find new students. Dr. Norton's vision of the modern woman may have included, but was certainly not limited to, that of a well-educated homemaker. Rather, his vision of a woman becoming what she should become was the catalyst for Keuka's early distinctive programs, which included business, economics, and law, as well a core of liberal arts.

The first edition of the *Keuka College Record* in January of 1921 further reflects the progressive ideas Dr. Norton had for the education of the twentieth century woman. In this and other documents from the times, there is frequent reference to meeting the stresses of life in its complex relationships. There was also a clear acknowledgement that life's work and pleasures were a dynamic adventure which, for men and women alike, required an education with specialization after the student is grounded in the fundamentals. Both the B.A. and B.S. degrees offered to the entering class of 1921 describe Keuka's long-standing commitment to the liberal arts while still providing ample opportunity for specialization. Thirty-eight women entered Keuka in 1921.

Although the relative conservatism which marks a Christian community prevailed at Keuka, there also appeared to be a high tolerance and encouragement for the spirit of innovation and change. This spirit would materialize in the form of new programs and initiatives over the coming decades. The next generation of leadership would transform Keuka from a self-proclaimed experiment to a credible woman's college.

Keuka's experiment is frequently referred to throughout the historical literature of the school. Several characteristics of the school are specifically referenced. First, there is the relationship of the college with the Park and the integrated nature of Keuka as a total community. Second, there is the blending of the liberal arts with the professional programs and the exceptional feature of field study, a form of cooperative education pioneered by Antioch College. Finally, there is Keuka's long-standing commitment to community service.

Keuka College: 1936-1970

Challenges and Opportunities for Growth

While Keuka continued to be a popular choice for many college-bound women during the early thirties, the institution was also coping with the increasing challenges of fiscal management. In addition to a growing physical plant and generally rising operational costs, Keuka had traditionally been a high student-aided institution. By the mid-1930s, shortly before Dr. Norton's resignation, the college was experiencing severe financial pressures. Even the faculty who had been fiercely loyal to Dr. Norton began to question the wisdom of some institutional decisions.

To the distress of some, particularly the remaining affiliates from the Free Baptists, Keuka was also beginning to attract more students from outside of the immediate region and even out-of-state residents. Although Keuka had long proclaimed its commitment to the children of the area, such a commitment was simply no longer practical. This was a particularly important turning point for Keuka. A shift from a local to a regional market would forever influence the nature of Keuka's programs and institutional ethos. By the mid-1930s, Keuka's enrollment reached approximately 200 students.

There was a tendency among some colleges during the Depression years to appoint young presidents. Locally, both Allegheny and the University of Rochester, as well as Keuka, would have young men at the helm who personified the progressive ideals of educational visionaries such as John Dewey and Robert Maynard Hutchins. Dr. Norton's successor, J. Hillis Miller, would not only perpetuate Keuka's long-standing commitment to a practical education but also saw to it that graduates were prepared to serve the needs of the greater society.

Keuka's Progressive Period

The next decade was a progressive period for Keuka.

President Miller introduced many new ideas for expanding the role of students and faculty in a variety of decisions, including curriculum and campus life. Dr. Norton's vision of educating young women to cope with the multitude of challenges of a changing world was about to blossom.

The profile of the students and the faculty were also changing. As previously noted, students were coming to Keuka from a broader region and more diverse backgrounds. It has also been noted that by 1937, Methodists and Presbyterians combined, as well as a much smaller number of other denominational backgrounds, outnumbered Baptists in attendance. Faculty were coming from a wide range of institutions and were less inclined to live on campus. Dr. Miller also believed in a more relaxed set of social rules, allowing for even greater opportunity for student interaction on and off campus. Although still rather strict by today's standards, alumnae from this era report many opportunities to build relationships with local boys, some of whom they ultimately married and settled with in the area.

With the coming of a new president and a cadre of institutional leadership in 1941, there also originated an idea which may well have been the single most important strategic decision Keuka has ever made. The combination of three variables--a new board member who held a similar position at Antioch College, the continued encouragement for colleges and universities to be progressive in programming, and a new president--led to the creation of field period. Although many colleges today have extended the concepts of career education to actual field experiences, Keuka was one of the first small liberal arts schools to establish a formal program. Keuka's nursing program was also introduced during this period. Eleanor Roosevelt had actually suggested this idea to President Miller, in part because of the severe shortage of wartime nurses. The nursing program, which eventually became one of Keuka's largest and best-known offerings, was also seen as an opportunity to take advantage of both state and federally supported subsidies. This decision, along with the new field studies program, gave Keuka an even greater vocational focus.

It would be eventually said that Keuka's nursing program and its early focus on teacher preparation would hurt the school's ability to build a badly needed endowment as these programs produce graduates who enter low-paying professions. Consequently, even if there was a more concerted effort to develop alumni as donors during these earlier years, the potential was weakened by the nature of Keuka's programs.

These were also difficult times for the campus as the school was still coping with managing an increasingly complex infrastructure. While student enrollment had grown to 225 by 1941, the somewhat idealistic communal world which Keuka had created for itself was actually beginning its decline.

Growth and Expansion of the Campus

Over the next fifteen years, Keuka would see its first woman president, Katherine Gillette Blyley, as well as significant expansion of the physical plant. Like much of the rest of the country, Keuka was enjoying a postwar lift in spirits. With an increasing enrollment and on-campus activity, both the college and the surrounding Park were growing together.

Keuka, like most colleges during this era, would also experience an influx of military veterans. Accepting servicewomen meant relaxing some academic standards and traditional entrance requirements. This was done in response to a national effort to provide educational opportunities for returning veterans. By 1946, Keuka's enrollment had grown to 436 students, creating a strain on the physical facilities and the already overworked faculty.

President Blyley's genuine love for Keuka was transformed into an unwavering and tireless commitment to the growth of the institution. While much of Dr. Blyley's presidency was devoted to fund raising and constructing new facilities, she is also best remembered for having spearheaded Keuka's Plan of Education for Social Responsibility. In retrospect, this plan not only created a formal vehicle for Keuka's commitment to social responsibility but also a means for the small school to draw even greater attention to its unique programs.

The Cold War period brought great anxiety to the nation, yet even small schools such as Keuka were reaching out to build a new world order. Under President Blyley's leadership, the number of foreign students enrolled at Keuka increased considerably, as did the number of study abroad programs being offered. One such program was the Keuka World Emphasis Sequence designed to:

> provide students with the opportunity...for first hand experience with the international scene and...direct acquaintance with people of diverse social and cultural backgrounds.[5]

An illness prematurely ended Dr. Blyley's tenure and created a period of confusion and poor management of the institution. The relatively frequent changes in leadership from this point forward had a detrimental impact on the school's ability to maintain a stable vision and focus on the future.

The Peak Years

Dr. William Spencer Litterick became the eleventh president of Keuka in 1959. Careful not to criticize his predecessors for their administrative decisions, Dr. Litterick nonetheless quickly informed the board that Keuka was not keeping pace with the rapidly changing educational and social climate of the country. At the curricular level, the new president was strongly committed to the liberal arts and immediately launched an effort to develop a new core.

Dr. Litterick also inherited a deficit which was reported to have grown to $100,000 and a physical plant which was beginning to show the stresses of poor maintenance and overuse. Like many colleges which experienced rapid growth following World War II, there did not appear to be adequate planning for the on-going expenses of maintaining the facilities. While today many colleges incorporated these anticipated expenses into their fund-raising, the costs of new buildings were not factored into institutional planning in the 1950s and 60s.

There was also a growing tension between faculty and administration. Like many campuses, Keuka was struggling with defining the increasing role of faculty in institutional decision-making. Through Dr. Litterick's encouragement, a faculty committee was established to draft Keuka's first constitution. It quickly became a point of controversy when Litterick claimed the committee had infringed on his powers as president of the institution. He was further incensed by the board of trustees' agreement with the faculty to discuss matters of the college directly with them, creating the possibility that the president could be bypassed.

Dr. Litterick may have been Keuka's first president to recognize that while modern colleges required the application of sound management practices to survive, these ideas were in conflict with the traditional infrastructure and norms for decision-making. Although Dr. Litterick is credited with having established Keuka's credibility among small private liberal arts schools, it was not without a price. Keuka's transition into a modern college with all of its implications, both positive and negative, had come to full fruition. Enrollment had increased rapidly throughout the 1960s (Table 3-1) but was about to reach its peak.

Decline and Recovery

Keuka College: 1970-1983

By 1970, Keuka's enrollment had peaked at 858 students, and administrators as well as the faculty were feeling optimistic about the future of the institution. There is little evidence that either group anticipated what would happen in the near future. The progressive movement of the college and amicable working relationship between administration and faculty in the mid-to late 1960s would erode rapidly over the next three years. One of the more popular presidents ever to serve Keuka, Dr. Wayne Glick, would see a major shift in enrollment and campus temper.

By 1973, Keuka's enrollment had dropped to 599 students, and a state of financial exigency was declared. As seen in Table 3-2, enrollment steadily declined until 1984, which marked the beginning of the recovery years. A variety of factors contributed to this rapid loss of students. One most frequently cited by the senior faculty themselves was the changing social and economic conditions. A weak economy, social unrest due to the war in Vietnam, racial tensions, and the feminist movement would all affect the types of students as well as the attractiveness of this small conservative campus.

TABLE 3-1
KEUKA COLLEGE
ENROLLMENT 1955 - 1970

Year	Enrollment	Percent Change
1955	328	
1956	349	6.4
1957	363	4.0
1958	338	-6.7
1959	367	8.6
1960	447	12.4
1961	534	19.5
1962	544	2.0
1963	648	19.1
1964	733	13.1
1965	724	-1.2
1966	745	2.9
1967	819	9.9
1968	810	-1.0
1969	844	4.2
1970	858	1.7

Net Growth from 1960-1970--92%

Source: Keuka College, September 1983, Self-Study Report

TABLE 3-2
KEUKA COLLEGE ENROLLMENT 1970-1994

Year	Enrollment	Percent Change
1970	858	
1971	800	-6.8
1972	668	-16.6
1973	599	-10.3
1974	586	-2.2
1975	580	-1.0
1976	594	2.4
1977	573	-3.5
1978	534	-6.8
1979	561	5.1
1980	544	-3.0
1981	524	-3.7
1982	500	-4.8
1983	444	-11.2
1984	420	-5.4
1985	435	3.6
1986	484	10.9
1987	524	8.7
1988	596	13.7
1989	550	-7.7
1990	650	18.2
1991	708	8.9
1992	808	14.1
1993	824	2.0
1994	905	9.8

Source: Office of the President, 1994

While Keuka would not become a coeducational institution again until 1985, a few individuals were beginning to question whether a women's college could survive. From the late 1960s until the final decision in 1985, the question of whether Keuka should become coeducational was occasionally discussed. In 1970, at one of the most critical times in the institution's history, a presidential committee again recommended against such an action.

Several faculty also recall a resistance on the part of the president to expand the offerings of professional programs at Keuka such as business or physical therapy, which would have better positioned the school for changes in market demands. The lack of vision on the part of administration to anticipate these changes combined with a general insistence on maintaining the single-sex status for another decade cost Keuka dearly.

The demand for education programs, one of Keuka's mainstays in the early 1970s, would experience tremendous decline. Between 1970 and 1985, the actual number of baccalaureate degrees awarded in this field, nationwide, declined by 34 percent. Nursing, Keuka's second most popular program during this period, was prospering in other institutions. While Keuka's enrollment was steadily declining, the number of degrees awarded nationwide between 1970 and 1985 increased by 178 percent.[6]

The next two presidents, Dr. William Boyle and Dr. Elizabeth Shaw, could not reverse the rapid decline of the institution. As presidential leaders, both were ill equipped to deal with the market forces as well as a campus community which was struggling to recognize that radical changes were necessary if Keuka was to survive. In many respects, the community was in a state of denial and simply not facing up to the fact that their institution was slowly dying. At one point in 1983, Keuka was literally hours away from closing when decisive financial actions were taken by the Board to remain open for one more year.

Keuka's strategic complacency during this period was, at least in part, due to its inability to recognize that many of the decisions which had been made throughout the school's early history were timely and in concert with the changing external environment. To survive, Keuka needed a new leader who recognized this axiom of institutional management. Keuka also needed a leader who understood that successful modern colleges required a sense of direction, fiscal discipline, and an appreciation for the unique characteristics of an academic institution.

Dr. Arthur Kirk was appointed president of Keuka College in the latter part of 1983. The records reflect that he assumed the presidency with an institutional debt of $350,000 in interest on a 1971 federal building loan and an institutional pattern of consistently operating with deficit budgets. In fact, the institution had lost over $2,000,000 over the previous ten years, half of that amount between 1980 and 1983.

For the first few years of his presidency, Kirk had virtual autonomy in determining the strategic direction of the institution. He wasted no time in making his position and intentions clear with the entire community. In one of his early presentations in which he discusses the topic, *Change Under Stress: When Traditions Must Give Way,* he points out that:

The president is a leader, and manager; articulates

a vision, makes it happen...has authority over everything; shares responsibility with faculty on educational policy and curriculum; and does not relinquish final authority...delegates effectively to administrators--or fails to be an effective manager; they serve at his pleasure.[7]

His style may have changed somewhat since these early years, but few, if any, would say he has wavered on the principle of presidential leadership.

In one of his first major addresses to the college community in January of 1984, the president reminded the faculty, staff, and board that they had failed to properly manage and lead Keuka out of this crisis. He believed that "Keuka lost the sense of its market and mission in the 1960s, was deluded by the baby boom; collapsed when the external environment did not guarantee growth; and, reacted to compensate for its problems, rather than address them."[8]

The new president publicly proclaimed his belief that while he expected the board, administration, and general community to accept change and redirection for Keuka, the alumni, students, and faculty would do so reluctantly. He saw the faculty as his greatest challenge and characterized them as having a distorted belief that "their authority transcended shared governance to absolute control."[9]

In reality, only during relatively short periods of time has the faculty had considerable control or influence over major institutional decisions at Keuka. These times have generally been during a period of weak leadership. While there is a myth in higher education, particularly among these small schools, that faculty possess significant institutional authority, it is generally not true. Oftentimes, obstructive behavior is misconstrued as having authority or control.

According to one faculty member, Dr. Kirk was given a great deal of latitude in his early years because that was needed to save the college. He recalled that, "We lost people because the romance of being a liberal arts institution was replaced with the reality of being a liberal arts based institution and being able to hold professional programs."[10] This fundamental shift in the programmatic emphasis, along with the decision to return to coeducation, set Keuka on a recovery course almost immediately.

Mobilizing the Community

Dr. Kirk, along with a reconstituted administrative team, immediately set out to develop and implement a recovery plan. The plan called for a vigorous initiative to stabilize and increase enrollments, increase revenue and reduce expenses, improve campus life, and rebuild academic programs. Within six months after his arrival, the entire campus was mobilized to tackle the crisis. In addition to the administrative team, the various faculty committees, academic leadership and even students were, in some fashion, involved in the review of the proposals. A review of the numerous documents and minutes from faculty and committee meetings during Dr. Kirk's first year would suggest that the new president did seek and receive a high level of participation in all major decisions. He did not, however, seek consensus. In virtually all major decisions affecting the future direction of the institution, the faculty had an opportunity to react and recommend but not to determine the final decision on any given issue. Even Dr. Kirk's relationship with the AAUP, which had been resurrected to deal with the problems of the last administration, appears to have been amicable.

By May of 1984, a special task force of board members, senior administrators, faculty, and alumni were appointed by the president to develop a strategic plan for the institution. The amount of time devoted to this initiative seems inadequate for the task at hand as the final report was submitted a mere two months later. The pace at which changes were suggested and actually implemented during this first year of the recovery certainly contributed to the eventual unrest among the faculty.

The report, while a thoughtful and carefully constructed assessment of the challenges facing Keuka, did not recommend that the institution return to coeducational status. By 1985, however, the recommendation was finally made at the administrative level. Today, virtually all of the faculty would agree it was appropriate.

By the fall of 1994, Keuka's enrollment reached over 900 students, the highest in its entire history. Through sound fiscal management, the administration has balanced the budget each year since 1984 while significantly improving the institution's net worth. Since 1983, the institution has maintained an aggressive fund-raising initiative, yielding approximately $15 million and building an endowment valued at $3.3 million as of December, 1994. These achievements exceeded the expectations of administration, faculty, and other constituencies, all of whom had worked diligently throughout the recovery period.

Initiatives Leading to Recovery

Action Plans

The incoming president announced a planned marketing approach to solve Keuka's problems and said he viewed higher education as "a specialized form of business." He further said, "The best (colleges) will always survive if they are well-managed. They must stay abreast of the market and manage the resources effectively. Colleges will survive based on the quality of their product-academics and education."[11]

Within two months after his arrival, Dr. Kirk and his administrative cabinet had drafted a five-year recovery plan calling for aggressive initiatives in the areas of enrollment, finances, physical plant, student services, institutional management, curricular revision, faculty professionalism, morale, governance, administration, and technical support. The new president made no attempt to conceal what brought Keuka to this state of crisis. In the report, he frequently points to Keuka's own internal problems, including poor leadership and failure to act under changing economic and market conditions.

The recovery plan, along with specific recommendations which followed over the next several months, appears to have been generated by this central group and did not include the general faculty. The one exception is the Task Force for Strategic Planning. In examining the gradual yet progressive recovery initiatives which Keuka experienced over the ensuing five years, it appears the president and his administrative team did provide a framework for institutional direction so badly needed and absent in the previous leadership. The president's model of involving the greater community in decision-making, particularly the faculty, was at work. He sought participation but did not allow himself the luxury of wasted time to make decisions and often set self-imposed deadlines for closure on a given item.

An examination of Keuka's current state of operations shows that the president's aggressive initiatives in all of the major areas identified in the 1984 Recovery Plan have proven successful. The initiatives since 1984 included enrollment growth of 115 percent; the college's long-term debt reduced by $3 million, the capital campaign netted over $11 million within the first ten years with a steady pattern of sustained giving ever since, improved physical plant with complete renovation of a major building, student life programs and all support functions properly staffed, the administrative areas completely reorganized, the curriculum redesigned with a strong liberal arts base, faculty/student ratios brought to fiscally responsible levels, and campus morale improved.

At the same time the Recovery Plan was created, the president issued a proposal for a calendar change, effective the following year. There had been an on-going debate over the inefficiency and outmoded calendar configuration for a number of years prior to his arrival. Best described as a modified trimester, the president sought to establish a calendar which better supported the current program strengths of Keuka. The institution's inability to reach a consensus on a new calendar had essentially hindered recruitment, and the college failed to act on the changing demands of the market. The old calendar was costly and inflexible.

The change in calendar, which now more closely resembles a traditional semester format with a lengthy break for Field Period experiences, was accepted without any controversy. Dr. Kirk reported that, upon his arrival, he asked the administrative team, "What is the one thing that everyone (the faculty) can agree on?"[12] While a need to change the calendar had been debated for years, previous administrations simply had not structured a decision process to bring the question to closure. The president refused to hold any open meetings on this subject but relied on small groups to discuss and structure the change. Dr. Kirk today feels that by not allowing any open meetings on this particular issue, he prevented a few disruptive individuals from stopping a long overdue change.

Within three months of Dr. Kirk's arrival, some of the most difficult decisions regarding academic programs were made. An Academic Program Direction Plan was issued by senior management, with the faculty curriculum committee, division chairs, and student senate having an opportunity to respond. Within one month after its distribution, the president and his cabinet concluded that majors in music, drama, philosophy and religion, dance, art, and history would be eliminated. Most full-time faculty positions were not jeopardized by this action as those teaching these subjects would be eventually redeployed to service the core liberal arts requirements. In fact, another astonishing accomplishment of this transition period is that no significant employee dismissals took place. With the exception of some adjustments in administrative staff positions, no faculty were laid off in spite of the financial exigency.

On the question of academic programs, Keuka has made a full shift to a liberal-arts based institution over the past decade. But in doing so, it has relied heavily on programs such as occupational therapy and business studies to generate enrollment. According to President Kirk, occupational therapy was actually one of several programs being considered by Keuka as long ago as the early 1970s. Now considered Keuka's flagship program, it was an overlooked opportunity twenty years earlier.

Controversial Initiatives

Among the academic issues which periodically surfaced during the president's first year was an on-going discussion over the creation of a women's studies program. The decision to return to coeducational status had not yet been made, and many of the faculty were still considering how to position the institution to be more competitive among colleges for women. Perhaps due to an undercurrent of sentiment that the institution should abandon its single-sex status, the push for a specific program in women's studies did not seem to gather much momentum.

The board, largely influenced by the president, made the final decision to abandon Keuka's single-sex status. This was not a decision fully welcomed by the community. Some members of the faculty report today, that those who really could not live with the decision simply left. There was little evidence that the return to coeducation had any negative affect on alumni relations. In fact, Keuka's successful fund-raising initiatives and rejuvenation of alumni are testimony of the support of this constituency.

The Role of Faculty

At the February 3, 1984 faculty meeting, Dr. Kirk reminded the faculty, success was contingent upon no one assuming that the president can do it alone. He briefly outlined the faculty's role in the recovery plan initiatives. Although the minutes reflect a more consensual model for making decisions, he did impress on everyone the need to move expediently.

Throughout the remainder of Dr. Kirk's first year, the faculty were not only active but eager to participate in the process, regardless of the manner in which decisions were ultimately made. A new academic dean was selected with the faculty playing a dominant role in the search. It would appear the faculty and community as a whole were pulling together to bring the institution out of the crisis. Enrollment immediately began to recover.

In general, the faculty's role in the numerous decisions made during these early years was clearly reactive rather than proactive. The president was not only setting the pace but also the agenda. Many of the faculty have said they were willing to allow this to occur, as they recognized that difficult decisions had to be made without a great deal of time for debate. Nearly all of the major recovery initiatives, including administrative and programmatic restructuring, greatly contributed to Keuka's return to a healthy status.

Not until December of 1984, exactly one year after Dr. Kirk's arrival, do the records begin to reflect a growing uneasiness on the part of faculty with respect to their role in decision-making. Much of the interaction between faculty and administration during the first year centered on programmatic and structural changes in the institution. By 1985, the shift in discussions was toward improving working relationships and personal welfare of the faculty.

In many respects, all of these early initiatives and the manner in which they were developed, shared, and acted upon set the stage for the working relationship which would evolve between the president and the faculty. The president, to this day, appears to be more comfortable with a relatively small inner circle of select individuals. Such groups, which typically include members of the faculty, are responsible for initiating change, seeking feedback from the community but using their best collective judgment in making recommendations. Some say that the president, who had final say in most matters during the early years, still does today.

The Strategic Positioning of Keuka College

Keuka Students

An examination of Keuka's successful turnaround in enrollment is a study in strategic marketing. Led today by an experienced professional, who reports directly to the president, Keuka's approach to the market is polished and effective. The professionalization of Keuka's admissions office has contributed a great deal to the recovery. Attractive and appealing promotional material stresses but doesn't overstate the liberal tradition, and the image is one of a close-knit community and career oriented programs in applied learning.

Claiming to work within a budget which has been relatively stable over recent years, the Admissions Office carefully targets the type of student it wants to attract and then aggressively goes after them. According to the Dean of Admissions, his department's initiatives have also been greatly enhanced by working smarter in the market and utilizing new techniques such as telemarketing through volunteers. Currently priced below their competition, Keuka markets their financial aid assistance "right up front," according to the Dean of Admissions.[13] The discounting of tuition is a common practice in higher education today, and although Keuka does not claim to apply any higher percentage of campus-based aid than the competition, they do a better job of making students and parents aware of what is available.

One might think the academic standards and integrity of the curriculum would have been compromised during the low enrollment periods of the early 1980s. This point was discussed at length with faculty and administration. It is a credit to the faculty and students that Keuka's programs remained academically rigorous, even during the severe enrollment decline.

The school's resurrection of intercollegiate athletics was also an important step in the recruiting of male students. One staff member estimates that at least 70 percent of all male enrollees participate in intercollegiate sports. The athletic staff, which spends considerable time in student recruiting, is intricately linked to the efforts of the central Office of Admissions.

An issue which surfaced in several interviews with faculty was the perception that athletes, more than any other student group, are given special status. One individual said, "We have an athletic director who is a Division III school and acts like he's at Division I."[14] It is also widely known that the president is a vigorous supporter of the athletic program, unlike the faculty in general, resulting in occasional tension. This said, it is also apparent that Keuka could not compete with area schools without such a program. It does provide a necessary ingredient of student life on a campus which one member of the faculty described as both "geographically and culturally isolated."[15]

Students are recruited from both rural and urban areas, primarily within a 200-mile radius. By focusing their energies on students who fit Keuka's profile, the admissions staff can seek out the students who would find both the programs and campus life appealing. With the exception of the students who come to Keuka specifically for one of the premier programs, such as occupational therapy, it is the campus and people themselves which attract students.

While an investigation of enrollment trends in the small-school sector indicated there have not been major fluctuations over the past decade, Keuka has experienced phenomenal success in recruiting. Applications and entering classes over the past several years have regularly exceeded national norms. According to a spokesperson at the Council of Independent Colleges, many of the small liberal arts schools have maintained at least a steady enrollment throughout the 1980s, primarily because of their continual movement towards offering professional programs.

Interviews with individuals from a number of schools in the area competing directly with Keuka indicated their institutions have held enrollments steady at best. While a number of these schools have traditionally maintained much larger endowments than Keuka, none attempted to launch major capital campaigns throughout the tight economic period of the 1980s.

Alumni

Keuka's fund-raising initiatives in the 1980s have raised the institution's awareness of and expectations of alumni. When the college embarked on its aggressive capital campaign, administration realized the importance of this group as a valuable resource. In the words of one senior administrator:

> Many of the alumnae thought of themselves as wonderful, nice, old, but poor school teachers, nurses and social workers. They're not. They're diverse, powerful women. Some with very good means, but we never held a mirror to them. So they never knew how good they were.[16]

What was discovered when the mirror was held up was that many of Keuka's graduates are quite successful and hold professional positions in law, medicine, and business.

Alumni, locally and nationally, have been mobilized by the Office of College Advancement. Through the efforts of this office, Keuka's alumni, particularly the women from pre-1983, are not only renewing their interest in the institution, they are also investing in its future. In a recent article in the *Chronicle of Higher Education*, Keuka College was showcased as one of the more successful schools in revitalizing its alumni as donors.

One graduate from the 1960s who typically gave $25-$50 to the annual fund is now pledging gifts of several thousand dollars. She characterized her previous modest gift as the equivalent of sending a dozen cookies. One factor which influenced her thinking about giving more to Keuka was the attitude that men, not women, are expected to give to college fund-raising. Keuka's Vice President for College Advancement says that while alumni have been typically generous with their time but not their money, there is now an awakening that the expectations have been raised.

The president has played a key role in institutional development. In fact, most believe it is his true strength. He spends a considerable amount of time working on fundraising and cultivation of new donors. Since Kirk assumed the presidency, alumni participation in fundraising has risen, as has corporate and foundation giving.

Keuka's Distinctiveness

In addition to the appealing lakefront setting of the campus and frequently cited secure and communal nature of the school, there are several distinctive features of Keuka College. Each has been an important factor, not only in Keuka's recovery initiatives but also in shaping the character of the school.

Keuka's shift from liberal arts to a liberal-arts based education has actually been occurring since the establishment of its nursing program nearly fifty years ago and even further back than that if we consider its historical focus on applied education. As is true for many other small private liberal arts schools, the gradual introduction of baccalaureate programs for specific career fields has often created the greatest controversy as well as opportunity for

Keuka.

When we examine the programs and number of students enrolled in each, it is debatable as to whether these schools should even be classified as liberal arts institutions. Keuka has maintained a broad-based general education requirement for all majors which includes coursework in ten different liberal arts disciplines.

While the liberal arts core is designed to complement and not compete with the professional majors, the working relationship among faculty in these distinctive programmatic areas is still developing. There appears to be a slow but gradual acknowledgement, even among the most senior liberal arts faculty, that small schools like Keuka must be willing to compete with other colleges and universities in the professional programs. In fact, one of its competitive advantages is the ability to assure employers that the students are educationally well rounded as well as technically competent.

Like many other competing institutions, Keuka has, in the past ten years, given increasing attention to the introduction of new professional programs designed to capitalize on shifts in market demands. One such program is occupational therapy. Now constituting the highest percentage of Keuka's total enrollment, it is almost solely responsible for the school's dramatic growth. No other program at Keuka comes close to this level of enrollment. Keuka is also currently enjoying an exclusive hold on the local market in this popular major as no other institution in the immediate area offers the program. It is also a high-demand field and students are easily placed in jobs after graduation.

The Education Division offers programs which have

also been some of Keuka's central and most popular professional areas of study. For decades, a large number of Keuka's graduates have entered the teaching profession and remained in the central New York region. Keuka is benefiting from a renewed interest in teacher preparation, and programs such as elementary education have nearly doubled their enrollment since the early 1980s.

A third professional program area, business, has changed configuration several times over the past decade but has experienced steady growth. Majors in business administration and management have been popular professional program areas for small liberal arts programs for several decades. There are a number of reasons for this, including the relatively low overhead for start-up and the natural linkages to traditional liberal arts disciplines in economics and the social sciences.

In addition to traditional majors in management, Keuka has launched other new programs such as food, hotel, and resort management. These programs can be more costly to operate than traditional business majors, and it is too early to determine whether this venture will prove to be successful. However, there are opportunities for academic programs such as this one to link with other institutional initiatives.

Over the past several years, Keuka has been operating an increasingly successful residential conference and seminar facility. It is not unusual for colleges to utilize their academic programs and students to staff and manage auxiliary enterprises, and there may be an opportunity to expand this venture. This venture has also contributed to the recovery because of its revenue-generating potential.

After fifty years, Keuka's field period program is not

only considered one of its most distinctive programmatic features but also a key selling point for attracting new students. Students are required to participate in a field period experience in each of their four years of study. Generally taking place during the mid-year January break, field period can be an individual or group experience, and, while the variety and type of opportunities has expanded over the years, the purpose of the program has remained the same. *The Student Handbook* describes the field period philosophy:

> Recognizing that the liberal arts curriculum is enhanced when it encompasses learning experiences both in and out of the classroom, Keuka College sets aside a period of time when all students are involved in experiential education opportunities. The purpose of the Keuka College Field Period is to offer students an opportunity to supplement their educational background and to enhance growth in personal maturity.
>
> This program is designed to link education with life experience by providing opportunities for awareness of social responsibility, cultural contributions and career possibilities. The faculty works closely with students in planning and preparation of Field Period, with the aim of strengthening and enriching their education.[17]

Students are required to establish learning objectives for each of the periods and whether a work or study experience, each must be approved and evaluated by a faculty advisor.

In interviews with senior administrators from three small private liberal arts colleges in the same region, each was asked what it considered distinctive about Keuka. All responded that field period was one of the primary characteristics which set Keuka apart from the competition. Keuka introduced experiential learning early in its history and over many years has continued to build on its reputation as being unique among small schools in adopting this educational philosophy. An emerging challenge for Keuka is to continue reshaping the experience so that it complements the changing focus of its academic programs.

Public Relations

Throughout most of the early 1980s and particularly in 1983, local newspapers regularly reported on Keuka's declining enrollment and fortunes. The recurring question was whether Keuka would actually open for a fall class. In retrospect, it is astonishing that the small institution was able to attract any kind of entering class, when the newspapers reported institutional debts in the millions and the sale of numerous prime properties just to raise operating capital. Nonetheless, Keuka did survive this period, and by the end of 1983 the newspapers were reporting the arrival of President Kirk.

President Kirk's ability to work the media and project an optimistic vision, even under the most adverse conditions, is clearly one of his strengths. To begin to turn the tide on public relations, he said upon his arrival that, "Keuka may not be in a healthy financial state, but I've seen much worse. I'd rather focus on the future than on the past."[18] Having been publicly acknowledged as an expert in improving both productivity and quality in higher education through planning and sound management practices, his credibility as an individual who could lead Keuka out of the crisis was critical to the recovery.

The president's vision of Keuka having the potential to become a school of national consequence has been criticized by some, even to this day, as unrealistic. However, his ability to continually push the organization beyond its perceived potential has contributed a great deal to the college's extraordinary accomplishments over the past decade. Skeptics may dismiss the president's vision, but the convincing way he and others present Keuka leads one to believe in it. It is a contagious attitude and certainly was a factor in the willingness of individuals and other organizations to contribute millions of dollars to the capital campaign.

There has also been an effort to build closer ties with the local municipalities. After World War II, Keuka made little attempt to align itself with the interests of the nearby townships, particularly the small community of Penn Yan. Even though Keuka is one of the larger employers in the area, and many students attend from the surrounding region, there was no conscious effort to interact with the local people. Today, many of the senior faculty and administrators, including the president, are active in local civic organizations.

Since 1994, Keuka College has continued to prosper and aggressively respond to the external environment. In addition to double-digit increases in applications over the past several years, it has launched another $4.5 million campaign. As the enrollment has increased, the institution has turned more attention to the residential environment of full-time students.

Always fiscally conservative, Dr. Kirk continues to gradually build a stronger financial base for the institution and is developing a long-term fund-raising strategy. The president's priorities have remained the same for much of his ten years in office: quality, distinctiveness, and growth. Virtually all decisions are made with these three key goals in mind.

In Summary

Keuka's story is not only an inspiring one for any small school which believes in itself and what it has to offer students, it is also an example of effective institutional decision-making, particularly through troubled times. While it is clear that much of Keuka's success is due to strong leadership by President Kirk, there are other subtle yet powerful messages in Keuka's story.

Keuka's recovery was also due to the collective efforts of a community, one which had sustained itself for over one hundred years. Such academic communities are embodied in the history, values, traditions, and capacities of an institution throughout its existence. These characteristics of an academic community are passed down through generations of leaders, faculty, students, and even the public's perception of an institution. President Kirk recognizes that his forceful style of leadership prevails only as long as the community is supportive and genuinely concerned for the welfare of the college. The next chapter will examine this point and continue Keuka's story in greater detail.

CHAPTER IV
WORKING RELATIONSHIPS
AT KEUKA

This chapter will begin with a brief historical review of Keuka's changing organizational conditions and evolving patterns of institutional decision-making as the institution matured and faced new challenges from the marketplace. More substantively, this chapter will examine in greater detail the people and events which contributed to Keuka's dramatic recovery over the past twelve years.

By the early 1980s, the entire community was finally forced to confront the real possibility that the institution could actually close unless significant and immediate steps were taken. Keuka's story is not complete without this more detailed examination of how survival became truly a collaborative effort. As reflected in its ability to cope with change for over one hundred years, Keuka is illustrative of the belief that the well-being of a college community is often based on the contributions of both faculty and administration. While the new president is credited with leading the recovery, this chapter will more closely examine the role of faculty and their changing relationship with administration.

Historical Perspective

In many respects the evolution of faculty and administrative relationships at Keuka has mirrored that of other colleges and universities throughout the past forty years. The proliferation of faculty-based committees, senates, councils, and advocacy groups such as the American Association of University Professors (AAUP), developed in concert with the postwar expansion of colleges and universities. In the absence of a faculty union, the AAUP has been reactivated several times at Keuka. This has occured primarily during those times when the faculty have found a need to collectively express their views to administration. Over the past twenty years, it would appear the AAUP chapter at Keuka has worked closely with a long-standing faculty liaison committee in representing the interests of faculty. A corollary to the management movement in higher education has been an increasing formal relationship of faculty and administration; and even small colleges are affected by this phenomenon.

Postwar Period

As reported in earlier chapters, Keuka, like most other colleges and universities, enjoyed a slow but steady period of growth following World War II. Throughout these years, while establishing itself as a credible institution, Keuka also gradually began to struggle with the challenge of organizational management. Although their personal styles differed, former Presidents Miller (1935-1941), Allen (1941-1946), and Blyley (1947-1958) were the last generation of leadership to enjoy a high degree of autonomous decision-making, with relatively little question or challenge of their authority from the faculty. President Blyley was also the last generation of leaders at Keuka who experienced steady, unfettered growth during her term of office. Historical records reflect that it was President Litterick (1959-1965) who first sounded the alarm that

Keuka was not taking appropriate action to position itself for the future.

The fact that the College was becoming more complex to manage, coupled with a rising movement of protecting the rights of individuals, resulted in a rather swift departure from the previous concordant relationship between faculty and administration at Keuka. The 1940 AAUP Statement on Academic Freedom and Tenure, followed by the creation of additional guiding principles throughout the 1950s and 1960s, was eventually introduced and endorsed by Keuka's faculty and board of trustees.

The first faculty constitution was created during President Litterick's term in the early 1960s. It was one of many initiatives originated by the faculty which would help shape and define their role and responsibilities in institutional decision-making. In many respects, the faculty constitution became the first guiding document to formalize the working relationship between faculty and administration. Dr. Litterick recognized the challenges which lay ahead and was one of the first presidents to express concern with whether the faculty and administration would discover new ways to work together.

The Late 60s and 70s

It was during the G. Wayne Glick (1966-1974) and William Boyle (1975-1978) years that Keuka experienced its most dramatic shift in patterns of decision-making and acknowledgement of where final authority would eventually reside. As previously reported, Dr. Glick's presidency began with an outward appearance of high promise for the small college, and he is remembered as one of the most popular individuals to hold the office. However, shifting demographics, rapidly rising inflation, and Keuka's failure to be responsive in a changing market also resulted in a state of financial exigency by the time his term as president had ended. It is interesting to note that when faculty today recall better days and a more collegial decision-making environment under President Glick, they fail to recognize how poorly the institution was doing in his final years.

As evidence of his commitment to participatory management, President Glick invited the faculty council, established in 1965, to participate in a long-range planning exercise designed to examine key elements of Keuka's continued growth. A document was produced which reviews a number of strategic issues including calendar, program configuration, continued status as a college for women, and even decisions which affect institutional finances and the physical plant.

During the Glick years, Keuka established three standing committees to deal with emerging institutional issues: the professional standards committee was established in 1968 as a formal body to act on the appointment of new faculty as well as assure the maintenance of high academic standards; the faculty liaison committee was established in 1971 to act as a conduit for faculty to administration, on matters of grievance; and finally, the curriculum committee was established in 1971 to assure the faculty's role in management of the curriculum.

President Glick's style was sharply criticized by the next administrative team which inherited the state of financial exigency, as well as an expectation on the part of the faculty that they would have a strong voice in virtually all aspects of institutional decision-making. In addition to the committees and the faculty council previously mentioned, the sixties saw the establishment of separate faculty groups--instruction, field period, teacher preparation, admissions and student personnel and guidance, college community social board, committee on financial assistance, and a committee on public events. In addition, another standing committee was established to oversee the Library.

By the early 1970s, faculy were so involved in overlapping committees and special work groups, all presuming a preeminence in institutional decision-making, the result was a period of confusion, inefficiency, and lack of true accountability for anyone. It should also be noted that most committees, with the exception of those which dealt directly with the faculty, such as the professional standards committee, also had students serving on them.

President Boyle recognized the problem of a burgeoning bureaucratic infrastructure at a critical time in the institution's history. His vision of a more streamlined organization, along with the immediate declining enrollment of the early 1970s, resulted in what could best be described as a near reversal in the working relationship between administration and faculty.

For the next ten years, including Dr. Shaw's presidency, much of the interaction between administration and faculty would be conducted largely through formal channels, including the local chapter of the AAUP. Records from the late 1970s, and up to the point of Dr. Shaw's departure, reflect a gradual acknowledgement from the faculty that their once-strong voice in institutional decisions was eroding.

There was a growing distrust of administration. It was also a period of weak leadership, and faculty were eventually forced to take charge of the institution, a posture they claim to have held until the arrival of President Kirk. As was earlier reported, it is true the faculty were certainly influential in Dr. Shaw's decision to retire from office prematurely. Dr. Shaw's inability to manage the crisis of the institution is well documented in spite of the apparent support from select members of the Board of Trustees.

The faculty were deeply involved in administrative affairs of the institution for much of the late 1960s, throughout the 1970s, and into the early 1980s. As the institution began to lose its strong position in the market, there was increasing attention paid to long-term planning, restructuring, and financial analysis. When reviewing historical records, it is much easier to understand the strong sense of ownership of the institution expressed by some members of the senior faculty during interviews. Many were personally involved in these processes.

While several individuals interviewed believe that faculty forced the resignation of Dr. Shaw's predecessor, Dr. Boyle, there are conflicting accounts on this point. It is true that Dr. Boyle did resign shortly after the faculty successfully galvanized their dissatisfaction with the president and requested the board remove him from office. However, there is no evidence that the Board actually removed either of these presidents from office, and the faculty's perception of their influence on the trustees is in all probability an overstatement of reality.

Transition Period

Final Confrontation with President Shaw

By the middle of the 1982-83 academic year, any semblance of a working relationship between Dr. Shaw and the faculty had deteriorated to its lowest point. In February of 1983, the faculty began a series of actions which not only contributed to the president's departure but also influenced their future perspective of authority in institutional decision-making. This perspective would resurface later in their developing relationship with Dr. Kirk.

On February 25, 1983, the faculty unanimously voted to establish an ad hoc faculty coordinating committee to create a representative body for faculty to be directly involved in institutional planning for the upcoming year. Although tension between the faculty and administration had existed for quite some time, this action was the most assertive initiative to assume control of decision-making.

Dr. Shaw did not initially object to the creation of the committee, which she viewed as potentially supportive and advisory to her role in formulating a strategy to deal with the immediate enrollment and financial crisis. However, Dr. Shaw did strongly object to a second motion which would create an ad hoc group directly involved in all aspects of institutional planning and finances. The president viewed this second action as allowing the faculty even greater authority, undermining her role as chief executive officer of the institution. In the meeting in which these motions were discussed and voted on, the minutes reflect the following:

President Shaw warned the faculty that the worst blow to the college would be internal dissent and...expressed grave concerns with the second motion. She stated that the faculty is really requesting the Board of Trustees to assign to an ad hoc committee of the faculty responsibility for oversight of all institutional planning for 1983-1984. She found the second motion to be so profoundly and finally rejective of the present administration that it would be totally inappropriate for her or any member of the administration to be part of the discussion or part of the action. President Shaw gave the gavel to Dr. White and left the faculty meeting followed by members of the administration.[1]

The records show that the faculty did establish the committee and were subsequently involved, at a detailed level, in examining the financial condition of the institution. By this time, any sense of authority or control over the situation that Dr. Shaw had earned over her term in office had deteriorated to the point of no return. The animosity which had been building between her and the faculty over the previous several years prevented any rebuilding of the working relationship.

By July of 1983, Dr. Shaw announced her retirement and much of the remainder of the year was devoted to continual efforts to avoid panic among students and the general community. Although Dr. Shaw remained active for the first half of the academic year and even served on the presidential search committee, she left immediately upon Dr. Kirk's arrival in January of 1984.

The Search for a New President

In early August of 1983, Keuka's Board of Trustees requested the faculty to select a representative who would serve on the search committee for a new president. The search for a new president began immediately. When asked today, the faculty believe they had adequate participation in the presidential search process, and the records do indicate they had considerable influence in the selection of Arthur Kirk.

Although the exact number of candidates recruited is not available, Dr. Kirk is aware of the fact that several other individuals were considered. The faculty liaison committee asked the faculty to be prepared to discuss and determine the criteria for presidential candidates at an upcoming meeting. This faculty liaison committee submitted the following recommendations for that review:

- Commitment to fund raising. We must have a person with the attitude that the most important task of the President of Keuka College is fund raising.
- Experience in fund raising. We need to increase corporate giving and foundation grants to the college. Depending on the skills of the new director of development, this criterion may be important for the President. While we need a person who would be attractive to our current strongest supports, we need a person who can also tap new sources of funding.
- Commitment to a liberal arts college. We need a person committed to a strong liberal arts core as well as strong preprofessional programs. We need support for liberal arts majors and for full-time faculty positions.

- Commitment to a college for women. We may want a person who can objectively and realistically assess the viability of Keuka as a college for women. If Keuka is to remain a college for women, we must have a person who can support this type of institution in the areas of recruitment, fund raising, and women's studies programs.
- Youth. Dynamic, energetic, achievement-oriented, experienced administrator, who verbalizes recognition and acceptance of challenges the position represents.
- Fiscal management. Provides evidence of the genuine understanding of a budgetary process. Can design a budget, appraise the college community of its fiscal condition, monitor and manage the budget to maintain fiscal viability.
- Commitment to accountability. The president must hold people accountable for their performance in the jobs they are supposed to be doing.[2]

The criteria were among the items discussed at the September 2, 1983, faculty meeting. The discussion centered on whether Keuka could find a new president who would view the financial situation at the institution as manageable. In part, this question was in all probability driven by the on-going debate with the incumbent president, Dr. Shaw, as to the severity of the crisis at Keuka. Earlier in the meeting, the Faculty Liaison Committee Chairman challenged the president's position that finances were in a relative state of stability, as were her projections of the number of students required to balance the budget for the upcoming school year. Much of the debate between President Shaw and the faculty was centered on the issue of short-term versus long-term survival.

In retrospect, the faculty's concerns on this issue appear to be warranted and a more realistic assessment of Keuka's situation than that of the president. Their perspective was longterm, while the president was focused on the immediate future. As a result of the creation of the faculty coordinating committee, the faculty were now directly involved in institutional finances and very much aware of the magnitude of Keuka's problems.

Another item discussed was the criterion of youth for presidential candidates. It was ultimately decided such a criterion was inappropriate, and the recommendation was adopted without its inclusion. In spite of this action, Dr. Kirk was appointed to the presidency of Keuka at age 37, making him one of the youngest to hold the office in the institution's history.

In spite of the criticisms which would later be expressed by some with respect to Dr. Kirk's presidential style and priorities, the faculty would appear to have recruited the person they genuinely wanted. Financial matters and a commitment to accountability are among his strongest skills.

Recruiting Arthur Kirk

While several others were considered for the position, it appears the board was intent on recruiting Arthur Kirk. By Dr. Kirk's own account, he was only marginally interested in coming to Keuka when the board first approached him. Very much aware of the severe financial crisis confronting Keuka, at the time of his interview, his perspective of the institution was that "it was already dead, it just hadn't been buried."[3]

It is to the board's credit that they were willing to persist in recruiting Dr. Kirk. Five board members travelled to Pennsylvania to convince him to visit Keuka one more time before making a final decision. Dr. Kirk did return and found several factors greatly influenced his decision to assume the position of president in spite of earlier impressions.

Like many others, Dr. Kirk was struck by the beauty and the physical setting of the campus. While the buildings had fallen into disrepair and he saw them as disheveled, they nonetheless were solid and well built. He contrasted this to other campuses which had expanded their physical plant over the past several decades and were poorly constructed from the beginning.

What perhaps influenced him most was a series of meetings with both faculty and students during this second visit to campus. Dr. Kirk made the following observations from those meetings:

> It appeared to me the faculty were remarkably good...they were well prepared and good teachers.
> The field period came alive to me...its value and philosophy.
> Keuka had been doing a more than adequate job of educating students in spite of the problems.
> The bottom line is that I was struck by the place...the place deserved to survive.[4]

Dr. Kirk readily admits that there was certainly some ambition and ego involved in the decision. He was also flattered by the persistence of the board. His naturally competitive nature may also have had something to do with the decision to assume the challenge. His closing comment on why he came to Keuka was, "I also had completed the Philadelphia marathon five hours prior to closing the deal...the moment was right."[5]

While Keuka's plan for recovery was largely that of President Kirk, it is also apparent the actual implementation of these initiatives could not have occurred without the commitment and eventual support of the faculty.

When both the faculty and administration were asked what contributed most to the recovery, the answers varied. The president said, "A thousand reasons, mostly little ones, but I don't think we could have succeeded if we hadn't gone co-ed...also, Occupational Therapy became our flagship program."[6] Interestingly, one senior faculty member attributed it more to "strict financial management and a wholesale renewal of administration, particularly development and admissions."[7] While there is probably no single answer, in the final analysis it could have been what the president calls "the psychology of recovery."[8] The fact is, this community, driven by the faculty and a concerned board, wanted to recover and was not willing to allow the institution to close.

Another important point to be made with respect to Keuka's recovery is that Dr. Kirk forced the institution to engage in a close examination of its internal capabilities as well as its position in the marketplace. While he has always pressed the organization to reach for high goals, Dr. Kirk is also quite realistic about Keuka's potential. In this respect, he is the most important strategic player in the organization.

Profile of the President

Arthur Kirk earned a baccalaureate degree in history and a masters in administration and supervision from Kean College in New Jersey. He completed his Ed.D. degree in 1983 at Rutgers University, concentrating in organizational development.

Prior to his arrival at Keuka, Dr. Kirk held several positions in higher education administration, beginning with assistant director of the Division of College Development and director of alumni affairs at Kean College, from 1971 until 1975. From 1976 until 1979, Dr. Kirk was director of development and planning for Somerset County College in New Jersey. In these positions, he was successful in substantially increasing gifts and grants to both schools.

In 1979, he was recruited to the position of vice-president at Misericordia, a small, church-affiliated institution in Luzerne County, Pennsylvania. Like Keuka, it had also experienced dramatic shifts in fortunes over the past forty years. Responsible for operations and finances, Dr. Kirk was a member of an executive team which struggled to strategically reposition the school in the late 1970s and early 1980s. His own doctoral dissertation, *Strategies to Affect the Survival of a Small College: A Case Study*, is about that experience.

The dissertation reveals not only the challenges of directing faculty in a small liberal arts school through a process of self-renewal but also the resolve that leadership must have to sustain the initiative. In many respects, Misericordia's story is the same as Keuka's. The school was lacking a clear vision and mission, coping with disengaged and demoralized faculty and existing in a state of denial as to its position in an increasingly competitive market for students.

Dr. Kirk has expressed his regret at not having been more successful in engaging the faculty in the process of change and minimizing the morale problems. Nonetheless, Misericordia's management team, which included Dr. Kirk, succeeded in averting the institution from the brink of bankruptcy. This was accomplished by making many hard decisions, quite often without full consultation with faculty.

Acting in a key leadership role throughout this transition period for Misericordia, Dr. Kirk was instrumental in achieving the following: student enrollment was increased; operating surpluses were realized each year; the core educational requirements were strengthened; new programs were introduced; the first successful capital campaign was conducted and annual giving more than doubled; the institution's endowment grew five-fold; and new computing systems were introduced to both the academic and administrative areas.

Changing Roles in Decision-Making at Keuka

This next section will examine the structure, process, and participants which have influenced institutional decision-making at Keuka over the past decade. It will also illustrate that the balance between aggressive institutional management and the desire to increase the involvement of faculty can lead to new challenges for the college. What will be illustrated is the complex and resulting bureaucratic infrastructure which can develop on a college campus when the needs of multiple constituencies must be considered.

Keuka's Faculty Constitution

The first evidence of concern from the faculty regarding their role in decision-making came in December 1984, exactly one year after Dr. Kirk's arrival. In an effort to better understand the president's intentions for future decision-making and to possibly initiate a change to the faculty constitution, the professional standards committee (PSC) called for a meeting with administration.

The PSC meeting was called to: (1) raise the question regarding the president's understanding of, and commitment to the principle of joint effort and (2) specifically solicit the president's position regarding criteria, policies, and procedures for appointment and evaluation of faculty personnel. One year later, the records indicate an on-going discussion of the principle of joint effort and particularly the effectiveness of the faculty constitution in defining their role in institutional decision-making. In spite of considerable debate on these points, the faculty constitution, which was last revised in 1980 under the Shaw presidency, remained unchanged as of 1992.

The ensuing discussion on these two issues and whether the faculty constitution should be changed would clarify, if not fully satisfy, the faculty's understanding of the president's decision-making style. One faculty member suggested that the faculty did attempt to challenge the president's authority but only for a brief period of time. In 1985 and 1986, the institution was simply not on solid enough ground for faculty to begin raising issues which might jeopardize the recovery. The president's comfort with the existing constitution would prevail. The faculty, who from this point forward would continue to press for more involvement in institutional decision-making, were also not going to allow themselves to be obstructive in the recovery effort.

Defining Joint Effort at Keuka

The president's response on the issue of joint effort was an important action in his still-developing relationship with the faculty. The president acknowledged the faculty's rights and responsibility as a professional body to engage in institutional governance, including their prerogative of self-evaluation and guardians of professional values and standards. However, he also made it perfectly clear that joint effort did not mean relinquishing his authority and responsibility to manage the affairs of the institution.

The president defined the faculty's authority and responsibility as horizontal or functional, and shared by many groups on campus and his as vertical, formal, and final. He further described the role of the president, dean, and division chairs as administrative with a hierarchical reporting structure, beginning with the board of trustees. The faculty reluctantly concluded that the president interprets his leadership role as originating exclusively from the board of trustees, which is certainly an accurate, if not entirely palatable reality at most colleges and universities.

This position was challenged by the faculty on the basis of their own interpretation of joint effort which they pointed out, is a principle approved by the Association of Governing Boards of Universities and Colleges including Keuka's, and based on the assumption that the leadership role of the President is supported by delegated authority from the board and the faculty. Their interpretation of joint effort sees the president in a dual role--as the executive officer of the board and the chief academic officer of the faculty.

In this dual role, he could overrule the faculty only in exceptional circumstances and for compelling reasons which must be stated in writing--and the burden of proof is with the president. Their fear was that the president was free to exercise his managerial power unilaterally--and vertical authority can become very arbitrary and unjust.

This reaction to Dr. Kirk was largely driven by the faculty's historical role in assuming an assertive position with the former president, Dr. Shaw. Having clearly taken the lead role from the former president in saving Keuka, they were still attempting to retain that same level of decision-making control with Dr. Kirk.

In spite of the faculty's protests, there is no evidence that the president made any significant change in his style of decision-making until the Middle States Self-Study in 1991. With respect to the joint effort question, it should also be noted that the AAUP Statement on Government of Colleges and Universities allows for considerable latitude in interpretation of this issue. Keuka's faculty have accurately pointed out that included in this statement is a reference to the president's role being supported by the delegated authority from the board and faculty.[9]

At question is the degree to which a college president, who serves at the pleasure of the board, must accommodate the wishes of faculty. The joint effort statement also identifies the president as the chief planning officer of the institution...and "has a special obligation to innovate and initiate...the degree to which a president can envision new horizons for his institution, and can persuade others to see them and to work toward them, will often constitute the chief measure of his administration."[10] This statement gives the president the direct charge to effect change, provided he or she continues to have the general support of the community.

AAUP at Keuka

While most AAUP chapters would in all probability take a dim view of the president's interpretation of joint effort, their activist tendencies are often tempered by the realities of institutional health. Keuka was officially in a state of financial exigency for nearly twenty years, a period which not only includes the time when faculty questioned President Kirk's decision-making prerogatives and those of his three predecessors. Nonetheless, today, and in recent years at Keuka, an objective observer would say that the AAUP has served a meaningful purpose, perhaps even more so than the faculty themselves recognize.

Dr. Glick, who has been portrayed by many of the senior faculty and in this report as a strong proponent of faculty participation in institutional decision-making, was unquestionably committed to a local AAUP chapter. Even in the Boyle years, which have been generally characterized as a period of strained relationships, the records indicate a still active AAUP chapter which attempted to maintain regular communication with central administration on major institutional issues.

Throughout at least the final years of Dr. Boyle's term, the records reflect a constructive exchange between the chapter and the president, discussing issues of institutional finances, leadership and the challenges which lay ahead for Keuka. While formal and to the point, the letter exchanges also appear to be candid and absent of any malice.

Until recently, the AAUP chapter at Keuka had been in a relative state of inactivity. Not since the Shaw years, when the chapter became one of the vehicles for faculty to express their unrest with administration, has there been any perceived need or desire to maintain the organization.

Today, the AAUP presence on campus is steadily growing in membership and function. It may come as a surprise to some, but the reasons for its revival are not entirely driven by tensions over faculty governance. The brief but anxious confrontation between the president and the faculty on the issue of joint effort does appear to have contributed to a renewal of interest in the organization. Keuka's AAUP focus since that period of time would suggest a more comprehensive role than merely of guarding the faculty's interest in institutional governance.

Although one senior faculty member suggested that at small institutions, most of the faculty know the AAUP segment on governance backward and forward. There was no evidence of this at Keuka. To the contrary, with the exception of a few faculty, both senior and junior, the majority have little interest in the politics of governance. What most faculty want is a more moderate and constructive approach, which not only resolves conflicts with administration but also addresses issues of mutual interest. One member of the faculty felt the AAUP also provided a forum for diffusing issues. She felt the AAUP was:

> a good place to take the extremes, especially the radical extreme and bring it back into moderation.

> I think you need to express those radical views. I think we need to talk them through. But I think we also need to say to each other, hey, you're out of line...that even though that's what you want, it's not the collegial action to take. When two or three or four people are saying to an individual, tone it down, it's much more effective than if just one person tries to do it.[11]

This was an interesting perspective as it reinforced the position that the president and the faculty took with respect to the fact that fringe members are not highly tolerated by anyone at Keuka.

The AAUP chapter does remain in the forefront of the movement to increase the faculty's role in institutional decision-making. They have been active in making faculty more aware of the legal implications of financial exigency and advocating for the restoration of previously lost benefits. At the same time, they have also co-sponsored with the president's office a reception for faculty following faculty meetings, begun to address the issue of faculty workload, worked on an institutional policy addressing sexual harassment, and reinstated a mentor program for new full-time faculty to provide support in the areas of college and community resources as well as institutional policies and procedures.

Whether the revived AAUP chapter will maintain its state of peaceful co-existence with administration is difficult to determine. That will probably depend on a number of factors, not the least of which is how long Keuka will continue to grow and prosper. While the immediate pressures of institutional survival are diminishing, it is much easier for administration to tolerate organizations such as the AAUP.

The 1990s: Middle States Is a Catalyst for Change

This most recent self-study report is the most clearly articulated and public expression of the frustration felt by a large number of Keuka's faculty with respect to their role in institutional decision-making. Unlike many accreditation documents which typically lean towards accentuating the positive, this report was used, according to one senior member of the faculty, to get the president's attention. It succeeded in both achieving reaccreditation and getting his attention.

Even to the novice reader of such reports, it becomes quickly apparent there was a collective effort put forth by faculty to leverage the reaccreditation process. From the perspective of the faculty, they were approaching the process from a position of strength and they felt the institution was never at risk of losing accreditation. It was evident by most standard measurements of institutional performance that the school was well along in its recovery. As compared with other colleges, both regionally and nationally, Keuka was enjoying an unprecedented period of growth.

Nearly three quarters of the entire faculty were involved in the development of this report. One member of the faculty said it was:

> a conscious effort to get more people involved. Of course some people said they're throwing more work at us, but I felt the process was collegial.

There were, what seems like endless meetings talking about problems that arose, and I didn't feel that ideas and feelings were at all overlooked or put down...it was a very good process.[12]

Reaction to the final report was mixed, however, among both the faculty and senior administration. Within both groups, there were some who felt the community was too harsh on itself, and "individuals went crazy...and were rather sophomoric." Perhaps a more positive perspective from one of the faculty was, "The institution had to show its warts because the reaccreditation team would have found them anyway."[13]

For those who took a more constructive view of the final report, including the president and dean, it was viewed as an opportunity for the faculty to go through a "grieving period" and "forced people to confront the issues...and for faculty themselves to say things that they were afraid to express in faculty meetings."[14] It might be a surprise to some, but the dean, who has been criticized for not fully engaging faculty in decision-making, offered this perspective of what the self-study achieved:

I've now got both the Board and the President committed in writing to a process (of defining faculty involvement in decision making). I got the faculty to sit down and give me a list of what they think is important. They can operationally define what the problem is and what they really want to work on...then we'll send somebody off to work on it. We got more out of the process by simply going through this than is visible in the document. A lot of the problem that we had in the process is dealing with the issues. Yea, you say you want to be more inclusive but show us.[15]

When research for this case study began, the Middle States Report was just being completed and, for a variety of reasons, campus morale was low. The remainder of the 1991-92 academic year was a tense period in the relationship of faculty and administration. Among other things, an unexpected short-term financial setback affected institutional pay raises and halted a five year plan designed to bring faculty salaries closer to market levels. Staff received no raises, further demoralizing an already overworked and underappreciated faction on campus.

Several years later and after Middle States reaffirmed accreditation, the tone is quite different. Everyone has now had an opportunity to reflect on the report without the threat of losing accreditation. The process did serve to bring people together in a variety of ways. One faculty member expressed it best:

Self-study has provided an opportunity to revitalize the faculty. It certainly has provided an opportunity for more people to learn about this institution...more people understand where the college has been and where it's going, than has been the case for a long time in this institution. Five years ago things were happening so fast and decisions were being made that the faculty learned about it in the newspaper. Many faculty simply disengaged and didn't bother to try to be involved. I think what has happened in the last three years is that it has turned around. Faculty reengaged.[16]

Today, there is less tension on campus, but select issues remain to be addressed, and both the faculty and administration believe the work is just beginning on a more participatory decision-making model. One section of the self-study report, which captures the real challenge, reads:

> Nowhere in the self-study process did discussions become more animated than on the issue of governance...the strong leadership and authoritative decision-making style that the president brought to the recovery were essential in the early years of the presidency...the stage is set for a more inclusive decision-making process.[17]

The board of trustees, the president, and the faculty share a commitment to the principles of joint effort contained in the American Association of University Professors 1966 Statement on Government of Colleges and Universities. That commitment was never absent, even during the hectic experiences of 1984-86. What was absent was a common understanding of the principles in application. The self-study report provides that common view. The challenge which remains is to clarify and implement appropriate roles in the planning and decision-making processes of the institution.

Keuka's historical patterns of involving faculty in institutional decisions have been influenced by a multitude of factors, all of which have been discussed as this study has traced the evolution of its equally dramatic growth, decline, and recovery. Both administration and faculty have consciously entered a new era which holds high promise for a more productive working relationship. Will they recognize and constructively react to the obstacles which will eventually confront them?

The Trappings of Institutional Bureaucracy

It is important to understand the current formal structures for faculty participation in institutional decisions. In addition to the organizational hierarchy, there has been a considerable expansion in recent years of committees and special work groups. This is partly due to the increasing demands for review of academic programs and campus life issues, which are a direct result of the successful recovery. It is also due to a genuine attempt by the current administration to broaden the participation of faculty in a multitude of decisions.

The president has always worked closely with an executive committee consisting of the academic dean, the vice president of college advancement, the dean of admissions and financial aid, the dean of students, and the business manager/treasurer. This group would constitute Dr. Kirk's inner circle of administrators, which he uses to initiate and drive most major institutional decisions. Each executive has a number of people reporting directly to him or her, with the faculty represented primarily through their division chairs to the academic dean.

Little has been said about the role of the dean up to this point in the report, although it became apparent in reviewing Keuka's history that the charge of this important academic position has changed with each incoming president. If forced to generalize on Keuka's deans, we would have to conclude that this position has more often served at the pleasure of the president rather than acted as an advocate for faculty. The implications of this relationship are far reaching, particularly in the sense that faculty are forced to find other means to express themselves.

A Plethora of Committees

The college maintained five standing committees throughout the recovery period, most of which have existed since the 1970s and are defined in the faculty constitution--the curriculum committee, the faculty development committee, the faculty liaison committee, the instruction committee, and the professional standards committee.

Throughout Dr. Kirk's term, there has been a steady expansion of additional working committees. Such as the ad hoc budget committee, the ad hoc facilities planning committee, the ad hoc new employee orientation committee, the campus safety committee, the communications taskforce, the computer users group, the experiential education committee, the professional development committee, the sexual assault prevention committee, the transfer articulation committee, the special events committee, the 50th anniversary field period committee, and the ad hoc advisory committee on the 1993-94 Budget.

Two additional committees were formed in recent years, each of which set the stage for increasing faculty involvement in determining the strategic direction of the institution.

The Mission and Goals Committee

Formed in the spring of 1992 and charged to deliver a draft mission statement to the board of trustees at their October meeting, this committee, which included members of the faculty, executive staff, and board of trustees, exemplified Keuka's vision of joint participation. This group worked extremely hard and succeeded in assuring that all constituencies of the campus had an opportunity to influence the final version of the mission and goals statement.

In spite of their accomplishment, an eleventh-hour minor flurry of dissent among some faculty somewhat tarnished an otherwise excellent effort. At a faculty meeting just prior to the statement being presented to the board of trustees, a question was raised with respect to one last opportunity for input before a vote would be taken on its approval. Securing faculty approval was of paramount concern to the committee, as well as the administration, since the document would reflect a truly cooperative effort among the various constituencies on campus. The dissent, while short-lived and supported by only a small number of the faculty, diminished the opportunity for everyone's spirits to be lifted by a successful joint effort. A vote was taken, and the new mission and goals statement was formally adopted by the faculty.

The fact that a few individuals insisted on questioning the document after what appears to have been a most thorough exercise was unfortunate. A certain level of dissension on any given issue at a faculty meeting is commonplace and even healthy for an organization, provided it is not so excessive as to become destructive. Of greater interest than the discourse of the meeting itself was the reaction of the faculty to their colleagues who dissented. Privately, one member of the committee expressed frustration with the fact that anyone would question what appeared to be one of the most successful joint efforts of administration and faculty in recent years. After leaving the meeting, one individual said, "No matter what we do, they are never going to be satisfied."[18]

Plan the Planning Committee

Of all the committees recently formed to expand faculty's role in institutional decision-making, this one illustrates both the aspirations and frustrations of faculty and administration at Keuka. As a direct result of the faculty's open challenge to administration that their once-strong voice in institutional decision-making had been lost, a plan the planning committee was formed at the end of the 1991-92 academic year and charged with (1) defining how the college should go forth with strategic planning, (2) determining the composition of a strategic planning work group, (3) devising the schedule on which the group would operate, and (4) articulating how this group's initiatives would relate to other planning activities within the institution. Among its members were senior administrators, faculty, and even central staff.

The work of this committee was of no small consequence to Keuka's future and to the expected changes in the working relationship between administration and faculty. It was one of President Kirk's first major steps towards creating a forum for the faculty to participate in a comprehensive and meaningful way in major institutional decisions. While the work of many of the other committees have strategic implications, none had greater potential for influencing institutional direction than this group. It was confronted with a formidable challenge. As the charge implies the Committee will discover the elusive formula for establishing and integrating a strategic planning process which everyone accepts, feels a part of, and which is not disruptive to other initiatives. As evidenced by previous research, few schools have succeeded in accomplishing this objective.

By the end of the 1992 calendar year, this committee, while only in existence for approximately four months, was experiencing a number of problems. To a degree, the problems were those raised by their colleagues at the summer retreat at which this planning initiative was launched. The retreat, which involved all of the faculty, specifically addressed roadblocks to planning and was designed to openly express concerns and propose solutions for a successful initiative. The following are some of the problems raised by the faculty at the retreat:

> Rapid growth of the institution...can't keep pace with the change.
> Lack of trust among faculty, administration, and even students.
> Lack of resources to carry out initiatives.
> Apathy and morale problems on campus.
> Lack of adequate training to engage in planning.
> Organizational chaos--who does what?
> Work overload--time not available to plan.
> Personal styles affect working relationships.
> Everyone's failure to communicate.[19]

The plan the planning committee, was not routinely communicating with the faculty on their progress and appeared to be working in isolation from the community. Since this period, the college has engaged professional help in developing a strategic plan with the faculty's continued involvement. Both the administration and faculty have continued to work together constructively, due at least in part to less pressure resulting from the highly successful recruiting and fund-raising initiatives of recent years.

However, there is a real hazard for the institution as all of the above-mentioned committees continue to proliferate and layer the organizational bureaucracy. This point was discussed with Dr. Kirk, and he is very much aware of the fact that Keuka went through a similar period under his predecessor, Dr. Glick. We know from our historical analysis that Dr. Glick, in his attempt to create outlets for faculty involvement, also created a situation where the institution could not make decisions rapidly.

Of greatest concern, and an issue which prompted the formation of yet another task force, is an ongoing concern with communication. The president appointed a communication task force in October 1992, charged with looking at this one barrier to successful planning.

Challenges of Communication

While effective communication has been a challenge at Keuka, as it is on most college campuses, there has been considerable improvement in the amount and quality of information being shared campuswide. However, the appointment of a communication task force was acknowledgement that a great deal of work was yet to be done. It should also be noted that at least half of the currently existing committees at Keuka have strategic implications on the direction of the school, making it an institutional imperative that these faculty-based groups function effectively.

One would think that on a campus the size of Keuka, communication would not be such a major problem. There was a time, even in its more recent history, when communication at all levels of the community was unquestionably more open and frequent. Certainly if we look back to the 1960s and earlier, greater numbers of Keuka staff lived in closer proximity to each other.

In addition to the fact that there were more full-time teaching faculty, the campus and Keuka Park were thought of as one community. For many, there was virtually no separation between their role at Keuka and other aspects of life. People worked, socialized, and raised families together, and, at least during the more prosperous years, there was little need to be involved in administrative affairs. In general, faculty were not asked, nor were they interested in being swept into the management of the institution; therefore, communication with administration was of an entirely different nature.

It should be pointed out that this all began to change for Keuka in the early 1970s. The breakdown in communication between faculty and administration did not begin with Dr. Kirk. It began with the initial decline in fortunes for the college when the administration was forced to begin making hard decisions about individuals and the organization as a whole.

It is also interesting to note that thirty years ago such decisions were hardly ever only about individuals. An action on one person was an affront to the community. The gradual breakdown of the community, its implications on the perceptions of individuals, and eventually the character of the school has had a profound effect on the working relationship between faculty and administration.

Formal communication occurs in a variety of ways at Keuka. Given the number of committees and special work groups, it is difficult to imagine how each could effectively share information with the rest of the college. Monthly faculty meetings provide the traditional forum for standing committee reports. Unfortunately, a review of fifteen years of faculty-meeting minutes suggests there has been little dialogue. In a two hour meeting, it is virtually impossible to present reports from five major committees, cover new business, hear from both the president and the dean, and still have time to engage in an open discussion on issues.

Early in this project and even before the planning committee was launched, a member of the faculty was asked what forum was available for them to discuss strategic issues. He indicated the only existing forum was the faculty meeting. However, he did not feel it was necessarily the best forum, saying:

> when there is an issue relevant to strategic planning that needs to be discussed with the faculty. To this point in time, it can only be discussed on the floor of the faculty meeting, if you really want the faculty's collective understanding of the issue. When the faculty have questions and want to pursue a question about strategy, the faculty bring that issue up, but its almost like question hour in the British House of Commons. The President chairs

our faculty meetings and if we have a serious question, then we have to ask him.[20]

The fact that the president chaired the faculty meeting did come up in several interviews. A former member of the board even questioned whether such an arrangement might present a conflict of interest or perhaps intimidate the faculty so that they would not be entirely open with their feelings. This individual actually questioned the former president, Dr. Shaw, on this point and was simply told, "It's a Keuka tradition."[21]

Time is also a major obstacle to good communication. The organization is overloaded and people do not have adequate time to teach heavy course loads, participate on multiple committees, and genuinely reflect on what their colleagues are doing on behalf of the institution. It is a double-edged sword. Faculty want more participation, so more outlets are provided for them to have it, resulting in stress, poor communication, and sometimes little progress. How does a campus allow itself to get to this point? One faculty member's explanation was that, "Administration uses structural solutions to solve personal problems."[22]

This was not only a plausible, but also thought-provoking observation of why Keuka and other colleges often simply form another committee to deal with a problem. Unfortunately, most organizations, including Keuka, do not invest the appropriate time in analyzing and determining the root cause of a given problem. They simply rush to fix it.

There is also formal communication directly between administration and the faculty through an academic council, consisting of the dean and division chairs. The council meets at the pleasure of the dean, and while it should be an opportunity to link administrative concerns with those of the faculty, it is not considered an effective working group. Again, there was inadequate time for a genuine exchange, and, at least until recently, the dean's relationship with many of the chairs had been tenuous.

At one point, the academic chairs formed their own committee of chairs, out of frustration in having to deal with administration and to provide a forum where they could share information and engage in discussions, without the dean's presence. Unfortunately, such an action would probably only serve to undermine other initiatives to improve communications. The real sentiment which led to the formation of this group is that there was sometimes not enough trust between the academic chairs and administration to work out issues in the presence of each other. This lack of trust was not only a problem for effective organizational communication but also in regard to other issues.

One final point on formal communication is worth mentioning. Even when the faculty have been instrumental in change, they might not have always been made aware of it by administration. One staff member, who also holds an academic appointment, said:

> I think the president would probably admit that there wasn't enough feedback to people to inform them of how the information they provided was utilized. That's real important. People need to be able to see that what they contributed entered into the final decision. Even if it's just a note saying, this was a good idea, I used it. Or a final report

that says these were the recommendations that were forthcoming and I used this and that, and here's the outcome of it...so that people can see that something made a difference.[23]

In many respects, the informal channels of communication are not only more prevalent than the formal ones but often more problematic. The political climate at Keuka, as is frequently found in many tightly woven organizations, can be intense. Strained working relationships are exacerbated by the constant pressures of increasing productivity with already stretched resources.

The only apparent cohesive desire of these individuals was to be somehow more in the loop of decision-making. None of these conditions is conducive to effective and productive informal communication. In fact, one faculty member claimed:

There are things that many of us believe, which simply can not be said in any public forum...for instance, you don't talk about the dead wood that exists...you don't talk about under-productivity.[24]

However, there was overwhelming evidence that when it came to working with students or supporting Keuka's overall program objectives, the level of cooperativeness and responsiveness among faculty was high. One member of the faculty put it as follows:

I think the informal links are excellent...in a time of crisis. If someone says, I know this is asking a lot but I really need to have this...people are just good about doing that and not saying, well, gee, that's not my job or my supervisor won't let me do that.[25]

The breakdown in communication, even at the informal levels, would appear to exist primarily on issues of administration and governance. On these issues, faculty ultimately must deal directly with the executive staff.

The executive staff, and particularly the president, has worked quite hard in recent years to both change any negative image and improve informal interaction with faculty. In interviews, several faculty said that if the president simply spent more time on campus, things might improve. Of course, Dr. Kirk and the vice president of college advancement did not lead the institution through a successful capital campaign and out of a financial crisis by spending more time on campus. There appears to be a lack of appreciation, if not a genuine naivete by some faculty, for the fact that the president's priorities have been primarily external, at least for his first eight years in office.

The lunch room, hallways, and seldom-frequented faculty club essentially provide the only forums for informal communication. The president also once hosted a monthly coffee hour, which, from two observations, appeared to attract little faculty interest. One individual reported that it is simply unrealistic on the part of the president to think that faculty are going to discuss any kind of substantive issues at a coffee hour which is also open to students.

Several faculty, including his otherwise strong supporters, were particularly critical of the president for not recognizing the ineffectiveness of this type of forum, presumably designed to promote more open communication. One individual indicated that all the faculty want these kinds of informal opportunities to meet and maybe even "bitch and moan." But she also said, that it would be inappropriate to "bitch and moan when students are there (the coffee hours), so nobody goes."[26]

Faculty report a marked decline in campuswide social affairs over the past twenty years, further eroding the strong sense of community and contributing to the distancing of faculty from each other and administration. While special events over the past year have helped to bring the different constituencies together in a more relaxed and informal atmosphere, there is no readily apparent answer on how to return Keuka to its once cherished communal environment.

The reality for Keuka as a college campus, like most families, is that it has grown, matured, and drifted apart. Keuka Park, which at one time provided a vehicle for many of the faculty and administrators to get to know one another on a highly personal level, no longer serves that role. One member of the faculty summed it up this way:

> We don't see the non-professional side of others; we only see the professional side, which we get to hate after a while. Lots of times, we meet somebody in a social setting and it changes how you deal with them on a professional level because you find out they're not the bastard you thought they were. We don't have any way to get to know each other socially...the older faculty will tell you that. They don't know anybody anymore. They used to know everybody and now they don't.[27]

In Summary

This chapter has illustrated the organizational conditions which affect and are a consequence of an institution's struggle to discover a more participatory decision-making environment. What is particularly noteworthy is Keuka's ability to survive and even thrive during this period of time, continuously re-examining the organization and coming to terms with the next threshold of change. This can be credited to both the faculty and administration, who, in spite of their moments of tension, have worked together for the good of the institution.

The increased formalization of the organization in recent decades also resulted in both faculty and administration redefining and clarifying their respective responsibilities. While Keuka has accepted, at least in principle, a number of the AAUP standards, there is little evidence either the faculty or administration are driven by them. With the exception of the debate over joint effort, these principles were never even mentioned in the many interviews conducted for the study.

The organizational structure and working relationships between faculty and administration are still evolving at Keuka. The institution should occasionally take stock of not only what it is accomplishing but also of what it is creating organizationally. Failure to do so may result in a far less-desirable working relationship than they may now feel exists.

Finally, beyond the obvious success Keuka has experienced in turning around its enrollment and regaining financial strength, this college can claim another important victory. While the element of community may have changed in recent years, it is still an important part of what this campus is all about. Perhaps, in the end analysis, this is what all colleges are about. A community of learning, living, and contributing to society is certainly what the small school has been for generations, and Keuka's story exemplifies it's capacity to excel without losing this critical aspect of it's organizational character.

CHAPTER V
WHAT SUCCESSFUL
SCHOOLS ARE DOING

The 1970s and well into the 1980s was a threatening period for all colleges and universities. A variety of complex and interrelated factors, including an apparent inability to cope with social and economic changes, left many institutions vulnerable, particularly those within the small private liberal arts sector. Many institutions would eventually experience a dramatic shift from rapid growth and a corresponding expansion of campus facilities to declining enrollment, fiscal constraint, and the burden of maintaining large infrastructures.

An atmosphere of skepticism swept the academy along with a strong sentiment that many institutions would not weather this period. This message was primarily directed at the small private liberal arts schools which seemed most vulnerable in the shadow of their publicly supported and larger counterparts in the university sector. In spite of the predictions that substantial numbers of these institutions would struggle and even cease to exist under the pressure, quite the opposite has proven to be true. A few did permanently close their doors in the 1980s; however, as a group, the small liberal arts school sector appears financially and academically stronger today than at any time in the past three decades.[1]

In recent years there has clearly been a heightened level of interest in the investigation of this phenomenon, as the response of these schools and their specific actions do provide valuable insight into the changing nature of managing colleges and universities through troubled times. The reporting of their survival has come in many forms, including research-based doctoral case studies, such as that cited in the previous chapters on Keuka College, scholarly articles, and even a few recent books. These publications profile specific institutions or provide an analysis of how innovative and aggressive leadership has successfully repositioned their institutions.

The following chapter is a reflection of this recent surge of interest and literature on the subject of small-school survival. It is also a result of an analysis of a cross section of small-school catalogs as well as first-hand accounts of five presidents and other senior administrators who are leading their own institutions through change.

Meeting the Challenges

By the early 1980s the turnaround efforts of these institutions were beginning to be noticed, and at least some leaders genuinely believed that opportunity was implicit in adversity, seizing the moment to develop a new vision for the future of their institutions.[2] Virtually all the institutions examined were facing the same conditions as they entered the decade of the 80s: declining enrollments, limited and even diminishing resources, a weakened public image, unstable administrative and management structures, and perhaps most damaging, a lack of direction.

In spite of the adversity, one individual felt that he and other small school presidents had one distinct advantage over their larger counterparts--the ability to act more swiftly and decisively. While there are many other characteristics of the small school which contribute to its ability to survive, this certainly is an important and identifiable one. In virtually all of the schools closely examined for this study, each exhibited an urgency in decision making and a willingness to take decisive action, even if it meant a short-term disruption to the organization.

As is true in all unstable organizations, the presence of strong leadership to direct, guide, and facilitate the process is an absolute necessity and generally desired by all internal constituencies. However, leadership alone, particularly in the academic community, cannot move an entire institution in a direction it does not wish to head. Such action also requires a willing and participative organization, prepared for the process of change, the uncertainties of the marketplace, and open to new ways of managing the institution.

Finally, the institutions examined were all proactive and simply did not allow themselves to ride out the difficult times. The passive or occasional reactionary measures of many institutions to change in the past were not seen as viable alternatives. A proactive and even aggressive posturing of these small schools in the marketplace has become one of their emerging trademarks.

Colleges and universities have, historically, been noted for not making dramatic and swift changes to the organization even under adverse conditions. Isolation and a sense of invulnerability have led many institutions to simply ignore impending crises. Academic institutions do have the propensity to survive long after any other enterprise might have collapsed. At least in part, this is due to the weak linkage between performance and accountability and is further compounded by the public's dependency and support of higher education in spite of the inherent weakness of self-management.

There is ample evidence that many small schools refused to face the reality that they were not making good decisions throughout the 1970s even while their enrollment and finances were gradually eroding. In contrast, those colleges which are enjoying successful turnarounds appear to be holding themselves more accountable to both internal and external constituencies. They do not expect nor anticipate anyone to take care of their problems. Arthur Levine, credited with the turnaround of Bradford College, said, "many schools have reacted (to hard times) by adopting a survival ethic, a myopic commitment to holding tight and riding out the storm of problems...this attitude is shortsighted."[3] Although Levine goes on to emphasize that focusing on institutional vision and purpose is of greatest value to long-term survival, most successful institutions still concentrate on the standard and easiest to measure performance factors: enrollment, general financial well-being, and public image.

It is primarily on these dimensions that the successful schools have focused their energies. They have done so through a comprehensive and often well-orchestrated process centered on strategic decision-making. To the credit of those small school presidents who have achieved significant gains in enrollment, financial well-being, and public image, it should be noted that each was also achieved by first creating a vision and sense of purpose for their institutions. In this regard, both long and short-term perspectives can be complementary and supportive of the overarching objective, institutional survival.

Within this context, we can examine those actions

which seem to appear consistently throughout much of the literature and shared experiences of small schools. In addition to the presidential interviews, the following conclusions were reinforced from a literature review and analysis of the catalogs, from scores of small schools throughout the country.

Thinking Strategically

With few exceptions, each of the presidents sees his or her actions as part of a more comprehensive initiative which can be captured under the aegis of thinking strategically. This includes a focus on establishing a vision and direction for the institution, conducting a thorough analysis of their strengths, weaknesses, and opportunities and finally, operationalizing these efforts into a plan of action.

One president felt it was his direct responsibility to effect strategic change in the institution, while faculty "sometimes see themselves as a body which will keep the administration from making a mistake." He, like others, would do so by first making the mission absolutely clear to all involved in the welfare of the school. Interestingly, it would appear that most liberal arts schools have not drifted from their founding missions and, in fact, have found new strength in adhering to those ideals which have sustained them for so long. For many, their fundamental commitment is still to undergraduate studies, excellence in teaching, communal environment, and a high quality liberal arts education.

One outspoken president said, "the train against the liberal arts is at full speed...the liberal arts people need to stand up and start screaming." When asked whether his school would compromise their strong commitment to the liberal arts for the sake of survival, he indicated, "absolutely not...we will not alter our mission for the sake of survival...we are not market driven!" The emotion and intent of the response was genuine; however, while his and other small schools may strongly believe they will not be market driven, in reality, many indicators suggest otherwise. Most successful schools are adapting their strength in the liberal arts to more creative programming which allows them to compete with other diverse institutions. In doing so, they have discovered the strategic advantages of their liberal arts roots and exploited them in the marketplace. It would appear many are being market driven.

A profile of five successful small school turnarounds in the mid-1980s probed this matter of market pressure and its implications on a liberal arts curriculum. All of these institutions faced the question of abandoning their long-held liberal arts tradition in favor of more technical programming. Each believed that their success in the marketplace was, at least in part, due to their commitment to the liberal arts. Their conclusion was that:

- First, the liberal arts are what colleges do best...it is the foundation upon which higher education is built. The vast majority of colleges have their roots in the liberal arts.
- Second, the liberal arts are highly versatile, offering colleges endless curriculum-building possibilities. Even the five schools profiled had very different programmatic features and offerings.

- Third, it is believed the liberal arts are the right education for the times. Based on a large body of research on the outcomes of a liberal education, the conclusion was that the liberal arts raise student capacity to adapt to changing environments. A liberal arts education cultivates the abilities required for work and for life - critical thinking, judgement, appreciation, values, communication skills, analytical, and conceptual ability.
- Finally, the liberal arts prepare students for a tough job market. The linkage between colleges and the world of work can be found throughout higher education's history in this country and began with those schools which uphold the liberal arts.[4]

Although fewer in number, some small liberal arts schools also have the same intensity for their religious roots and hold them as a highly regarded principle in their institution's direction. One president of a still thriving small Free Methodist sponsored institution admits that his strategic direction is more administratively driven, however, "all of our constituencies believe in what we are doing." This particular institution still requires church services three times a week and is relatively restrictive with respect to personal behavior of the students, and that of the faculty and staff. When asked how his institution can compete against the numerous other small schools in the area which essentially provide the same type of programming with far less control on behavior, he simply replied, "you would be surprised how many students (and parents) want this." It became clear this president had created a niche for his institution in a market which had abandoned such values in favor of a more liberal environment. This institution has strategically positioned itself as the school which embraced a set of values not found among the competition.

In literally every institution examined, leadership had made it a part of their strategic decision-making process to keep the institution headed in a direction that was clear to their internal as well as external constituencies. Asked how this is accomplished, one president indicated that faculty involvement was critical to the process, as faculty believe they "are the soul of the institution." He admitted to consciously creating an environment where only select faculty were involved, however, communication was open and frequent with the entire community. He also believed that there was genuine "wisdom in the larger" group and the "democratic" process could work in strategic decision-making. Finally, he stressed a point that was perhaps most important for all of academic leadership in moving faculty along in the same direction. He said, "rather than fight the question (of who governs the institution), force the solution...faculty must be willing to accept responsibility and obligation to decision-making, and we can only blame ourselves if we fail."

With respect to the strategic process, each of the schools examined reflected a similar concern for issues related to mission, constituent involvement in decision-making and utilization of precious scarce resources. In light of these and other unique characteristics of an academic organization, it becomes apparent that successful schools also create an environment which is conducive to the strategic process, yet not threatening to the ideals and principles of its various constituencies.

One of the earliest profiled cases of successful turnarounds was published in 1980. This study examined Birmingham-Southern College, a United Methodist affiliated institution which rebounded from rapidly declining enrollments, chronic deficit budgeting, poorly conceived programming, and a loss of public confidence. A gradual erosion throughout the late 1960s and early 70s was reversed within four years through an aggressive, well-orchestrated, and uniquely designed strategic decision-making process.

Defying the perspective that strategic management had to be bureaucratic, technical, and only the responsibility of central administration, Birmingham-Southern developed a plan which recognized the value of traditional management tools but placed a premium on participation of the entire community, consensus building, flexibility and creativeness, actions based on data, and responsiveness to a changing marketplace.[5] This formula, which can be seen emulated by a number of institutions working through their own survival strategies over the past decade, is a simple yet effective and realistic perspective of the academic organization.

Other institutions, such as Westminster College of Salt Lake City, were facing similar difficulties during this same time period yet took a more structured and unilateral approach to their strategic decision-making. Perhaps driven by a greater sense of crisis which prompted a declaration of financial exigency and even layoffs of tenured members of the faculty, their strategic actions were based on a consciously developed and articulated plan of the president. In this scenario, it was nearly an imperative for administration to take both an aggressive and deterministic approach to moving change along.

Characterized as an intensive planning exercise involving outside consultants, Westminster's case is also illustrative of the occasional need for leadership to assume nearly an autonomous role in turning well-conceived ideas into actionable initiatives. The financial exigency gave leadership considerable latitude to reorganize programs and redefine responsibilities, while rebuilding the school's financial base. Their efforts were successful, and by the late 1980s, the school was experiencing record-high enrollments and elimination of debts.[6]

Aggressive Marketing and Student Recruiting

Of even greater concern than their financial conditions was the gradual decrease in student enrollment, beginning in the late 1960s and lasting well into the 1980s. Because the schools are dependent on tuition for operating capital, the loss of even a few students can produce tremendous strains on the entire system, particularly over a sustained period of time.

In response, successful small schools have become quite aggressive in their outreach to the marketplace. Adapting many of the techniques promoted by educational strategists such as George Keller, author of *Academic Strategy*, the small liberal arts schools have discovered that they can be competitive. Of particular note and interest is the fact that the competition is not confined to their own ranks. By first capitalizing on their own unique characteristics and second, offering a greater variety of professional programs, many small schools are going after students who might have otherwise opted for large universities.

One president met the challenge of developing the market by convincing students that they would get their money's worth at his institution. This is essentially the same challenge that all colleges and universities face today, as most long ago shifted from a focus on selecting students for admission to recruiting. Simply put, it is a buyer's market, particularly among the small liberal arts schools where the range of reputation, costs, and programming is extensive. Since students have so many choices today in both programming and educational environment, every institution is faced with the same challenge.

Frederick Rudolph, a renowned scholar in the history of higher education and himself a graduate of Williams College, recently reminded us that institutions became providers of services and student consumers following World War II. This happened not by choice but through the sheer number of individuals who sought the service and the scope of opportunities available. According to Rudolph, as the system of higher education in the United States ballooned into a vast network of diverse offerings, students "developed a deeper awareness of their powers as consumers."[7]

From a strategic perspective, schools such as the one mentioned earlier, which claimed to not be market driven, have indeed learned to capitalize on what they can uniquely offer prospective students. By fiercely clinging to a traditional strong liberal arts programmatic foundation, this particular school genuinely believes it can maintain a distinctive position in the markeplace. It is anticipated that students searching for this type of education will make it the institution of choice. This strategy is much like that of institutions with strong religious affiliations which still believe they can maintain a niche in the market by exploiting particular characteristics of their educational experience, such as an emphasis on personal values and moral character.

All of the presidents interviewed have aggressive marketing and recruiting plans in place, typically with professionals at the helm of the initiative. A recent article in *The Chronicle of Higher Education* also revealed that some directors and deans of enrollment management, the more modern term for what we once called admissions, are beginning to command much larger salaries than their predecessors. Several schools reflected those individuals ranked among the top five highest paid professionals in the institution. The same holds true for senior administrators who hold positions in institutional development.[8]

Many of these schools have realized the need to rebuild all of their outreach initiatives through a professionally trained and full-time committed staff. One school had even gone so far as to abandon the traditional professional admissions staff who recruited on the road in favor of a contracted group of telemarketers. These individuals place telephone calls in the late afternoon and evening to all inquiries. Follow-up with good prospects is then carried out by full-time staff. This effort was further supplemented by college nights, a common practice among all institutions for recruiting new students. In this particular case, the school felt it had gone too far in merely striving for numbers. The focus on numbers had begun to affect both the quality of the students and their capacity to pay full tuition. Consequently, this particular school was considering abandoning its sweeping approach to the market in favor of more focused activity.

Of particular note is the level of sophistication which small schools have reached in getting their messages out through publications. For this study, and through an inquiry letter written as a prospective student, 57 program catalogs were solicited from schools in 22 different states. The letter simply indicated an interest in programs in the liberal arts. The only criteria for selection of schools was that they fall within the liberal arts classification of the Carnegie Commission and their enrollment did not exceed 2,000 students. Although it was not a forced distribution considered when selecting these schools, 22 of the 57 institutions (38 percent) represent schools with greater than 50 percent enrollment in the professional programs.

Without a single exception, all requested catalogs were received in less than one month after the inquiry, with nearly all of them arriving within two to three weeks. Many of the catalogs reflect the highly polished marketing approach schools are now beginning to take in their initial contacts with students. They are colorful, illustrate a wide range of program options, and a vibrant campus life and are quite obviously designed to entice a student to make further inquiries. Many, but not all of the colleges, also had several follow-up brochures and even telephone contacts.

A analysis of catalog content yielded a variety of consistent messages. The following messages, presented in rank order (number of occurrences), reflect what was found to be most frequently conveyed, in a consistently strong manner by more than 80 percent of the schools:

- Availability of financial assistance to incoming students.
- An education which provided personal and intellectual

growth.
- A high quality education.
- Low faculty/student ratio.
- Expressed community values.
- Strong liberal arts education.
- Active social and cultural environment on campus.
- Athletic programs.
- A faculty dedicated to teaching.
- Opportunities for internships and cooperative education experiences.
- Availability of academic support programs.

While there is some, but relatively little, reliance on the faculty to engage in the recruiting function, the new enrollment management professional does recognize the value of making a connection between prospective students and those with whom they will ultimately have the most contact. Direct contact with faculty typically occurs after the application process; however, in two schools examined, Augustana College and Wellesley College, the role of faculty is considered quite important in the student's final decision. Both institutions believe it is the faculty's responsibility to define the educational programming of the college, be prepared to articulate the values and character of the school and actively participate in the process.[9]

A willingness to be aggressive in the marketplace does not appear to have come easily to many small schools. Many have simply allowed themselves to become complacent in public relations and have not effectively informed the public of what their institutions have to offer. By taking a more aggressive posture, many other small institutions are discovering that they have the capacity to set their own course and posture in the marketplace.

In the mid-1980s, at least one institution, Franklin and Marshall, determined that its enrollment was only one factor in the overall well-being of the institution. The quality of the incoming students as well as their educational experience was also of paramount concern. For that reason, the school would not allow itself to be driven by numbers. In light of demographic shifts, of which they had no control, the long-term strategy would be focused on a smaller enrollment base with an even higher quality educational experience for those recruited. Rather than seeking more students, the focus became improved programming, recruiting the best students, and reducing attrition. Recognizing the market pool was shrinking, they would concentrate on gaining a higher share of the top-end students.[10]

Another institution, Incarnate Word College, made a conscious decision in the 1980s to find a better balance between economic, ethnic, and religious diversity in their enrollment. By reconfiguring its financial aid package, the school was able to attract more middle-income applicants, balancing out its current enrollment of low-income and high-income students. This shift in focus resulted in an increase of 1,000 students.[11] This practice of managing financial aid packaging as well as other creative financing mechanisms appears to be contributing to the turnaround of a number of schools.

One institution has begun to offer what could be characterized as a money-back guarantee for incoming students. St. John Fisher College, in upstate New York, announced it will pay $5,000 to each student who participates in a program labelled The Fisher Commitment and fails to obtain employment upon graduation.[12] This offer was first made to the 1994 incoming class. Such creativity, which some may suggest borders on gimmickry, nonetheless reflects the lengths that schools are willing to go to create a name for themselves in the increasingly competitive market for new students.

Public Relations and Fund-Raising

In concert with aggressive marketing and recruiting has been a new effort to increase public awareness of what these unique institutions have to offer. The objective is to project a stronger image to the public and also build the foundation for fund-raising. No longer a choice for survival, small schools have been forced to adapt aggressive public relations initiatives to compete for students as well as donor dollars.

One president, whose school, like many others, has turned to radio and television advertisements, indicated that getting these messages out to the public was an essential element of running the institution, as "the character of the school is changing as we grow and develop...we promote what we are doing, what we do well and what others don't know about." Successful schools recognize that they can not be stagnant in a dynamic environment, and the competitive conditions require them sometimes to be aggressive. They must be willing to try creative and perhaps even radical new ideas to get their messages out to the public.

In addition to needed renovation and expansion of long-neglected campus facilities, many small schools are discovering that the increased demand for financial aid has also created corresponding pressure to raise capital and improve their endowment portfolios. Consequently, building public image is often a prelude to fund-raising campaigns, and many small schools are adopting ambitious goals. In comparison to large universities, small liberal arts schools have traditionally maintained modest endowments, relying more on tuition dollars for their revenue stream, but over the past decade, small schools have shown what they are capable of achieving in the fund-raising arena. Several schools examined for this study, including Keuka College, illustrate the dramatic success of these institutions.

- Profiled in *The Chronicle of Higher Education* as one of the schools making a strong recovery in the the 1980s, Roberts Wesleyan, in upstate New York, reported an endowment which had risen from $220,000 in 1981 to $1.29 million by 1989. As of the beginning of 1995, the school reports over $5.5 million.[13]
- Over a six year period, Franklin and Marshall quadrupled their endowments to $60 million. This phenomenal success in fund raising is one element in their equation to improve the overall quality of the educational experience. By leveling off and even consciously reducing the number of students competing for financial aid, their endowment base has an even greater value.[14]
- Hobart and William Smith Colleges recently announced a $75 million campaign. The colleges' last campaign, which took place between 1984 and 1988, yielded an astonishing $27 million, when in fact their goal was a mere $13 million![15]

In Summary

The last three chapters have illustrated the potential small schools have for not only meeting the challenges of a competitive market but also for effectively managing their decision-making and long-term strategies. In many respects, Keuka College and the schools analyzed throughout this chapter represent the new breed of small liberal arts institutions. They have learned to both celebrate and capitalize on their rich history, heritage, and uniqueness as liberal arts institutions, resulting in a stronger position in the marketplace. In this regard, they are also an example to all colleges and universities of what can be accomplished when an institution applies itself to sound strategic decision-making practices.

The next two chapters are designed to provide a better understanding of the issues, opportunities, and constraints experienced by all institutions in their effort to redefine and redirect their decision-making. This section is also about managing change, which has become an unavoidable consequence of the competitive marketplace.

CHAPTER VI
EXTERNAL ENVIRONMENT

Change Variables in Higher Education

A System of Decision-Making

The previous sections of this book presented a historical perspective of higher education as well as a profile of small schools which have been successful in meeting the challenges of change. Their stories, while inspirational, are not complete without a deeper understanding of the conscious process of decision-making which must take place in order to achieve such success. The following two chapters will provide a framework for analyzing the external and internal variables which affect the health and welfare of all colleges and universities in today's competitive environment and, consequently, their decision-making process.

Others support the position of this book that small colleges which have discovered formulas for managing these environmental factors can not only survive but even thrive. Ruth Cowan is among those individuals who have recently presented the argument that small tuition-dependent colleges are not on the decline. Through her own investigation of small college recoveries, Cowan concluded, among other things, that success was mostly attributable to the internal actions of the institution.

Cowan referred to one common problem among institutions still struggling to discover their own formula for affective decision-making as patterns of problem-blindness. Patterns of problem-blindness refer to the blind spots that academic leaders have in analyzing their own institution. It is an inability to see and come to terms with those factors which are influencing the direction of the institution. This identifiable problem in decision-making among struggling institutions was further identified through a study by Paul C. Nutt and Robert W. Backoff, which led to the troubling conclusion that non-profit organizations, in particular, tend to use very limited information to define issues and make decisions.[1]

To reduce this pattern of problem-blindness, which may very well be endemic in all academic institutions, the following is provided to assist leaders in analyzing those factors many believe to be most critical to the future success of colleges and universities. Chapter VI presents a format for analyzing external factors that should be monitored and weighed as to their potential affect on the institution. Chapter VII, using a similar technique, will provide a method for considering those internal organizational factors which also must be taken into account by the institution.

Together, these chapters are designed to provide a systems view of institutional decision-making, which those responsible for the task can utilize to analyze their own internal organizational conditions and external position in the marketplace. While these chapters suggest a methodical approach to institutional decision-making, based on facts and data, the use of intuition and best guesses should not be entirely ruled out. The caution, as suggested by Cowan, is that this should not be a license to shoot from the hip as there has been such a tendency to do so in higher education decision-making.[2]

External and internal factors only become relevant in the context of the defined mission, goals, and objectives of the institution. Colleges are intrinsically different than for-profit organizations. Thus, care must be used in operationalizing goals and objectives. One significant difference is the role of internal constituencies in determining the direction of the organization. Faculty expect and should be afforded considerable latitude in their role as caretakers of the educational mission. However, this freedom should be exercised within the parameters of decision-making which also supports the overall direction of the institution.

This section of the book is designed to help the reader to understand the problems involved with the implementation of any action plan. The old axiom that a plan is only as good as the ability of its people to execute it, is one well worth considering in an academic organization. Certainly this is an important consideration of decision-making in small schools, which not only depend on senior administrators but also department heads and even faculty senates to operationalize plans.

Realities of the Marketplace

The legacy of Adam Smith is that organizations intent on gaining access to the needs of the public must focus on the competing forces of the marketplace.[3] Historically, the academic community has fostered a different perspective. Some believe, particularly those among the faculty ranks, that colleges and universities and, indeed, education itself, should not be subject to the dehumanizing influences of market forces.[4] Yet, as colleges have discovered, failure to address such critical issues as market forces can be, and often is, disastrous.

The mere mention of any conceptual framework that places administration of colleges within earshot of traditional business practices, such as strategic planning and decision-making based on an assessment of market conditions, has caused reactions from mild to strong disapproval from the faculty. At least until recently, many colleges have felt their direction should be largely influenced by the collective wisdom of the faculty as expressed through traditional decision-making bodies such as senates, councils, and influential committees. There has also been an admittedly arguable fear from faculty that bureaucratic manipulations by heavy-handed administrators will attenuate the educational process. For these and other reasons, acceptance of the principles of strategic decision-making has been slow within the academic community.

The reality for today's colleges and universities is that, like other complex enterprises, they do not exist in a vacuum. Thus, it becomes imperative in these changing times, as vividly painted by such educational scholars as Arthur Levine, to understand the external dynamics which will influence and even structure the growth pattern for educational institutions.[5] The major areas of study when scanning the external environment are normally grouped into the following categories: (1) economic; (2) social, cultural, demographic, and environmental; (3) political, governmental, and legal; (4) technological; and (5) competitive analysis. The primary objective for most colleges willing to accept the challenge of competing in an open market is to analyze each of these factors external to the organization in order to determine future opportunities and to be aware of impending threats.[6]

Economic Factors

Popular business periodicals, such as the *Economist*, *BusinessWeek*, or *Forbes*, provide us with a sense that variables in the economy can be monitored and perhaps even predicted with some degree of accuracy. However, James Gleick, in his national bestseller on chaos, discussed the futility of trying to make sense out of a myriad of economic conditions which affected our everyday lives. In attacking the world of economic forecasting, he says that "...economic forecasting by computer bore a real resemblance to global weather forecasting." Clearly, he was echoing the frustration of many when he said that "...econometric models proved dismally blind to what the future would bring."[7]

There is an argument to be made, however, that discernible economic patterns can be discovered when the methodology incorporates the unique conditions of the enterprise being investigated. For instance, in higher education it has become imperative to consider the costs of maintaining the institution in relation to what the market is willing or even capable of paying. Yet true costing models for program delivery in higher education are virtually nonexistent.

Economic trends can and do impact institutional operations, and astute financial officers are aware of this fact. One such set of indicators which reveal how economic conditions may have been creeping up on higher education is illustrated in Figure 6-1.

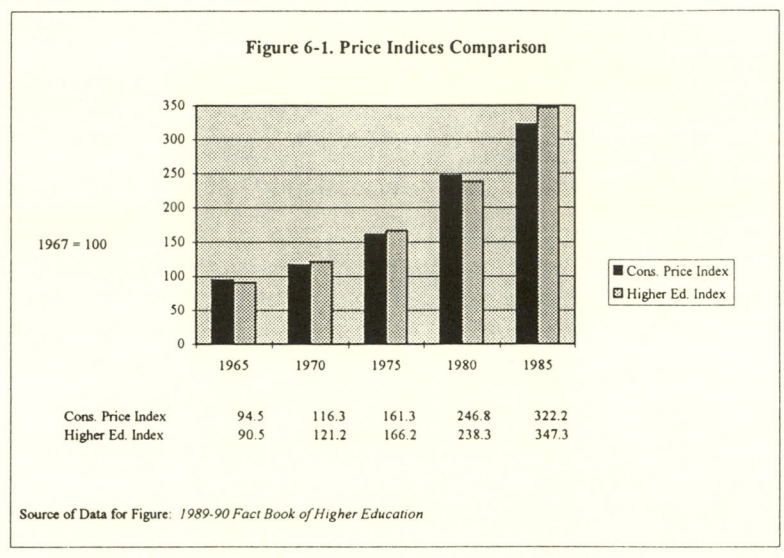

Figure 6-1. Price Indices Comparison

1967 = 100

	1965	1970	1975	1980	1985
Cons. Price Index	94.5	116.3	161.3	246.8	322.2
Higher Ed. Index	90.5	121.2	166.2	238.3	347.3

Source of Data for Figure: *1989-90 Fact Book of Higher Education*

The Consumer Price Index (CPI) is a monthly measure used to determine the change in prices of approximately 400 goods and services that consumers purchase.[8] The Higher Education Price Index (HEPI) measures the effects of price change on a fixed group of goods and services purchased by colleges and universities through current educational and general expenditures excluding sponsored research.[9]

Comparison of these two indices reveals that starting in 1970, the Higher Education Index has been generally outpacing the CPI. Consequently, not only does the parent of a prospective student have to worry about the rise in the cost of goods and services purchased in daily life, he or she is also confronted with the fact that higher education costs are outstripping the CPI. Unless parents receive a proportionate raise in annual income to counter the CPI, normally called the Cost of Living Allowance (COLA), their purchasing power will diminish. Adding an inflation factor to the HEPI, the discretionary income remaining for parents to send their children to college is now dissipated to the point that they may not be able to afford private schools. As Figure 6-1 shows us, this trend has been present since the 1970s. As a result, the pressure on parents to send their children to lower priced public institutions continues to mount. While this historical economic perspective is revealing, there is relatively little in the current literature on which economic indicators should be more closely monitored by colleges in order to predict future trends.

As for an environmental scan, each institution must ascertain which external economic forces have a direct impact on their operations in the short and long term. Since we know that the prospective student population is no longer homogeneous, each college must determine what it has to offer, what type of student is attracted to it, and perhaps more importantly, what is its capacity to afford this type of education.

These questions can only be answered through an internal assessment and must be addressed in order for an environmental scan to be conducted. With the institutional profile in hand, economic trends can be tracked in order to determine possible implications on the student-recruiting process.

Since the advent of economic theory, the profit sector

has been attempting to discover the formula which allows them to track those variables which will provide a glimpse of the future with some degree of reliability. Although no one such formula exists, most managers and planners admit that they must continue to monitor the environment in search of early warning signals for events that will impact their organization. The following are offered as examples of select key economic variables which may be useful for colleges to track.

- Availability of credit.
- Unemployment trends.
- Level of disposable income.
- Consumption trends.
- Income differences by region.
- Price indices.
- Interest, inflation, and money market rates.
- Gross national product trends.
- Governmental monetary policies.

Caution must be taken in placing too much trust in the world of the economists, especially when they tout birth rates as the key indicator. According to Levine and Associates (1989), "...the most important factor in projecting college enrollment in the 1990s will be the projection of college-going rates--specifically, projections of the speed at which the gap is closed between college-going rates of whites and those of disadvantaged minorities."[10] The lesson is that, although economic indicators are useful in understanding the external environment of higher education institutions, other external variables need to be addressed in order to gain a more complete picture of possible opportunities and threats.

Social, Cultural, Demographic, and Environmental

There appears to be some tension between demographic trends and the prospect for recruiting students to small schools. Analysis of Figure 6-2 reveals the dip in the number of eighteen year-olds in the 1990, which has caused many colleges, and particularly small schools, problems in meeting enrollment objectives.

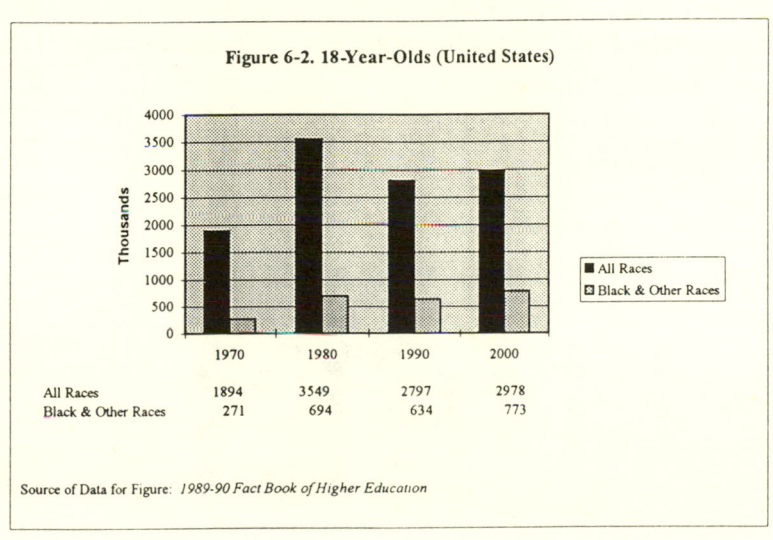

Figure 6-2. 18-Year-Olds (United States)

	1970	1980	1990	2000
All Races	1894	3549	2797	2978
Black & Other Races	271	694	634	773

Source of Data for Figure: *1989-90 Fact Book of Higher Education*

Projections   for the year 2000 show that the number of eighteen-year-olds is steadily increasing, however, not at the same proportion as in the pre-1980s era. The number of minorities are clearly on the rise: thus even though relief may be in sight for small schools, their traditional student base has changed.

To compound these issues even further, analysis of Figure 6-3 indicates that the expected population growth will not be in the East where a majority of the small liberal art colleges are located. The pool of students is shrinking and without a radical rethinking of how to attract eligible candidates, perhaps possessing an entirely different profile, the small liberal arts college will be competing in a declining market.

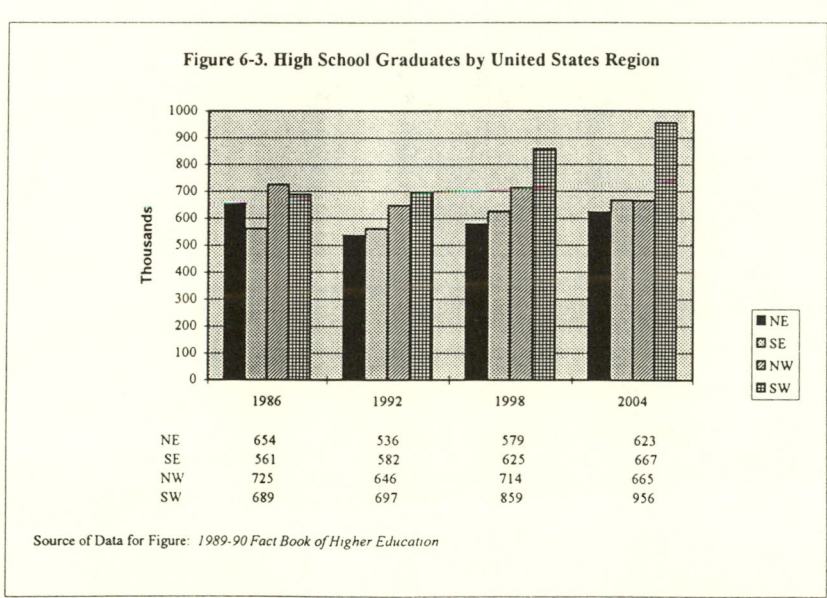

Figure 6-3. High School Graduates by United States Region

	1986	1992	1998	2004
NE	654	536	579	623
SE	561	582	625	667
NW	725	646	714	665
SW	689	697	859	956

Source of Data for Figure: *1989-90 Fact Book of Higher Education*

The small schools have also been more dependent on the student who meets the more traditional profile of eighteen to twenty-one years of age, and they do not have a history of programming which reaches out to what has become the growth area for college enrollment, the continuing education student. Figure 6-4 reveals that the 18 to 21 year olds, who are considered to be the traditional cohort for many small colleges, are no longer the only target group for recruitment. Through even this simple demographic analysis, it becomes clear to academic planners that their traditional student base has eroded. It is necessary for the institutions to make internal adjustments if they are to be attractive in the emerging markets.

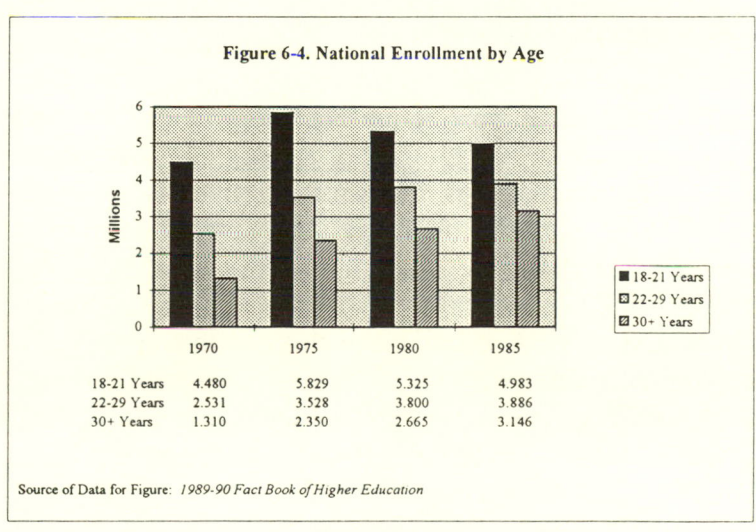

Figure 6-4. National Enrollment by Age

	1970	1975	1980	1985
18-21 Years	4.480	5.829	5.325	4.983
22-29 Years	2.531	3.528	3.800	3.886
30+ Years	1.310	2.350	2.665	3.146

Source of Data for Figure: *1989-90 Fact Book of Higher Education*

In addition to birth rates, other key social cultural, demographic, and environmental variables may prove useful for monitoring future expectations of students, particularly as they relate to the curriculum. The following is offered as examples of select social, cultural, demographic and environmental variables which may be useful for colleges to track.

- Rates of birth, life expectancy, and immigration.
- Per-capita income.
- Retirement trends.
- Changes in sex, race, age, and income.
- Evolution of social programs.
- Patterns of government intervention in social welfare.
- Lifestyles.

The concept of allowing market forces shaped by social and economic indices to influence curriculum design is not new to higher education. The current trends simply point schools into a new direction, and those capable of responding will continue to survive and some will even prosper. The small school may very well have a strategic advantage in getting ahead of the curve with respect to this new wave of environmental trends as their ability to react to market forces has been demonstrated throughout history.

In Table 6-1, college enrollments by racial and ethnic group reveals that between 1982 and 1991, overall enrollment increased by 16 percent. It also shows that the Asian and Hispanic categories had the biggest gains in college enrollment between 1982 and 1991. More importantly, as pointed out in all the data, the composition of the potential student body has changed enough that colleges can no longer rely on their once held view of the marketplace.

Table 6-1 College Enrollment Growth Rates by Racial and
Ethnic Groups between 1982-1991

Category	% Change 1982-1991	% of 1982 Total Enr.	% of 1991 Total Enr.	%Change Total
Native Am.	29	.7	1.3	.6
Asian	81	2.8	14.5	11.7
Black	21	8.9	11.9	3.0
Hispanic	67	4.1	17.6	13.5
White	9	80.7	50.3	(30.4)
Foreign	25	2.7	4.3	1.6
All	16	--	--	--

Source: Data used for the calculations taken from
The Chronicle of Higher Education Almanac, August 25, 1993.

Political, Governmental, and Legal

The effects of governmental programs on the operations of colleges are well documented. Government loan and grant policies, Affirmative Action and Equal Employment Opportunity statutes all have a direct impact on enrollment and the cost of operations for colleges and universities. These variables, coupled with the prevailing political climate in the country all influence the financial resources that will be made available from local, state, and federal governments to higher education. Continuing reduction of this resource at each level of government, applies pressure for colleges to seek additional financial aid.

As a case point, Bundy Aid was established in New

York State to help small private colleges absorb some of the shock of rising educational costs. Private colleges in New York were given a fixed stipend for every student who graduated. As pressure mounted on the New York State budget for competing programs, former Governor Mario Cuomo felt compelled to reduce the aid to private colleges through the Bundy Aid program.

Thus, colleges were cut 50 percent to 60 percent of the anticipated revenue that they were expecting from this program. Some colleges depended on this source of revenue in order to balance their respective operating budgets. While other, more conservative, institutions did not specifically count on this revenue, they wanted to use it as a quasi-endowment to be spent after receipt of the Bundy Aid. In either case, the financial position of the colleges was affected by the political environment in New York. Private college presidents lobbied legislators and Governor Cuomo in order to maintain their level of support from the Bundy Program, but to no avail. Colleges either did without certain projects these funds were to have been used for, or faced a disastrous situation if the funds were to have been a source of revenue in their operating budget.

Although colleges are generally tax exempt, tax rates, antitrust legislation, and trade sanctions all play a role in the ability of society to support education. Small private colleges are particularly vulnerable as they are dependent on endowment and annual donors. Alumni who are struggling with their own personal finances will be less inclined to provide the financial support that they would have in better times. Development offices on campuses need to track this data to determine what impact it will have on their fund-raising ability. Since most small private colleges cannot support themselves through tuition alone, corporate and alumni giving becomes critical if the institution is to support its current operation and continue to grade its programs and facilities.

Monitoring of educational lobbyist activities has become an increasingly important issue for private institutions. For example, of this point, in a 1994 issue of *The Chronicle of Higher Education,* Scott Jaschik describes the battle to save federal research funds for higher education. In the article, he states:

- The 1995 Defense Department budget is turning into a quagmire for higher education.
- The House of Representatives halved President Clinton's request for $1.8 billion in Pentagon support for university research.
- The lawmaker largely responsible for that cut... announced that he would hold hearings on the overhead reimbursements that universities receive for federally supported research.

Previous hearings on that topic have been a major embarrassment to higher education.[11]

Jaschik explains how lobbyists from large schools like MIT are working full time in order to regain the lost funds. One of the arguments presented by a lobbyist was that not only would loss of research funds affect the livelihood of tenured professors but it will, in turn, prevent graduate students from being mentored by these academic specialists.[12]

College and university planners and lobbyists must understand the need to monitor such variables.

Furthermore, they need to appreciate the systemic ripples that occur in organizations when seemingly unrelated activities occur within an institution. The loosely-coupled metaphor used by Weick to describe the organizational interface activity in higher education is sometimes misleading.[13] While college organizational structures can be as bureaucratically designed as a military unit or a manufacturing company, the interdependence between academic departments and staff departments is often misunderstood.

Lack of governmental funding for tuition assistance has a rippling effect on institutional finances. Subtle changes in enrollment invariably impact housing, food services, bookstore operations, and a variety of other income generating auxiliary services. For small schools, this phenomenon can be devastating, as their return on investments for sunk-costs is already modest in comparison to that of the larger institutions.

Although small schools have a difficult time making their needs known to legislators, it becomes incumbent upon advocacy groups to voice their concerns. Many of these schools have joined formal associations like the Council of Independent Colleges, Association of Independent Colleges, and Council for the Advancement of Small Colleges, while also forming local consortia to provide a collective voice for their positions. It is also imperative that they remain sensitive to the changing trends. The following is offered as examples of select political, governmental, and legal variables which may be useful for colleges to track.

- Special tariffs.
- Political action committees.
- Legislation on equal employment.
- Foreign pact arrangement.
- Government fiscal and monetary policies.
- Political conditions in other countries.
- Special local, state, and federal laws.
- Technology.

Technology is defined in the *Oxford American Dictionary* (1982) as "the scientific study of mechanical arts and applied sciences" (as engineering).[14] In 1993, a widely used college management textbook described technology as "the combination of equipment, knowledge, and work methods that allows an organization to transform inputs to outputs."[15] It is interesting to note that within the relatively short span of one decade, the concept of technology has expanded from the pure and applied sciences to a more inclusive perspective of how people organize themselves to achieve commonly-held objectives of the organization, whether it be industry, hospitals, or colleges.

With this expanded understanding of technology, small schools need to rethink their positioning in the higher education market based on their facilities, faculty expertise, and financial resources. A case in point would be the growing opportunity that exists in the recruitment of non-traditional students. New technology in higher education, such as the recent innovations in distance learning, has been largely due to this market phenomenon. Distance learning is also providing new opportunity and access to education for students with special needs, such as full-time workers, single parents who find it difficult to leave their homes, and students with physical constraints that make it difficult to get to campuses.

Another rationale Robert Jacobson gives for the dramatic expansion of distance learning is the unparalleled advance of information technology.[16] Two way videos, telecommunication, and interactive computer technology have stressed not only the pedagogy of the classroom but also forced educators to address the access versus quality dilemma.

Advancements in technology, which expanded the potential market of new students, have also created new problems. In concert with the advancement of technology, and thus access, is the increasing awareness that many students require additional support to both understand and retain new information. Schools of all sizes are being forced to develop programmatic opportunities for remediation, much of which is carried out in areas commonly referred to as teaching/learning centers (TLCs).

Two major problems have arisen in regard to the TLCs. First, although some students take full advantage of the resources of the Center, many are intimidated by their association with it. It appears to be a scarlet letter that announces to the world that this student is not fully prepared for college-level work.

Another concern is the challenge faculty must face in learning new pedagogical techniques and coping with a changing student profile. The advent of new technologies, which has resulted in greater access and a more diversely prepared student, poses formidable challenges for faculty. Each institution must consider whether they are truly prepared for the consequences of this phenomenon. Without a willing faculty, capable of making the inevitable transition, venturing into this arena of market opportunity could spell disaster. While planners within small schools strive to maintain their viability from a technological perspective, these opportunities also come with a price and must be studied in the context of other variables within the institution.

In the spirit of the importance of scanning the environment, an institution might ask itself the following questions in trying to determine the impact that technological advances will have on the school.

- What are the technologies within the institution?
- How critical is the technology to the institution and the various departments within?
- What is the status of development of these technologies in the external environment?
- What is the evolutionary path of these technologies in the near and long term?
- What has been the traditional investments in these technologies by the institution--both planned and actual?
- What has been the return on investment in these technologies?
- What is the cost of not updating these technologies-- both in the near and long term?

Alvin Tofler, in his 1971 best seller, attempted to awaken us to the forthcoming shift in power bases throughout a world society.[17] In *Powershift* (1990), he puts forth the argument that the technology of transferring information has replaced the smokestack technology of the

Industrial Revolution as the most critical factor in fixing power bases in our society.

> Today we are living through one of those exclamation points in history when the entire structure of human knowledge is once again trembling with change as old barriers fall. We are not just accumulating more facts--whatever they may be. Just as we are now structuring companies and whole economies, we are totally reorganizing the production and distribution of knowledge and the symbols used to communicate it.[18]

Small schools need to find their place quickly in this movement to a fully operational high-tech/information society--the Third Wave society, as Tofler would put it. English language already replaced German as the scientific language of choice and French as the diplomatic language. According to Altbach, "...the bulk of the world's scholarly journals are published in English and the Anglo-American universities spend more than half of the world's total academic budget for research and development."[19] Monitoring changes and investing in the technology of educating students must be a priority of small schools if they wish to continue competing.

Competitive Analysis

Many academicians have been a part of planning committees which attempt to articulate how their college is different from the competition. First, an attempt is made to use the mission statement to glean pearls of wisdom that will project to prospective students that we are different. It is often concluded that the college respects the dignity of human beings. In analyzing many catalogs, it also becomes apparent that many small schools project a caring, communal environment, while maintaining a high regard for scholarship in their approach to education. The discussions often wind their way to institutional costs, the quality of the curriculum, and student life on campus.

This scenario is illustrative of the fact that academic organizations routinely engage in various forms of planning and critical analysis processes. What is often absent in such deliberations is a clearer understanding of the competitive factors, which must be considered and weighed against these important internal conditions. In Figure 6-5, a schematic presents those factors that help define the intensity of the competition.

The external scan results are uncovered through an analysis of the economic, socio-cultural, political, governmental, legal, and technological conditions of the external environment. The opportunities and threats determined from the scan have a direct relation to the institution's current competition. Figure 6-5 is a visual indicator that reflects the reality that institutions are affected by the external pressures around them. Of course, institutions, in turn, often try to influence external factors by lobbying, for example, for increased funding and controlled costs.

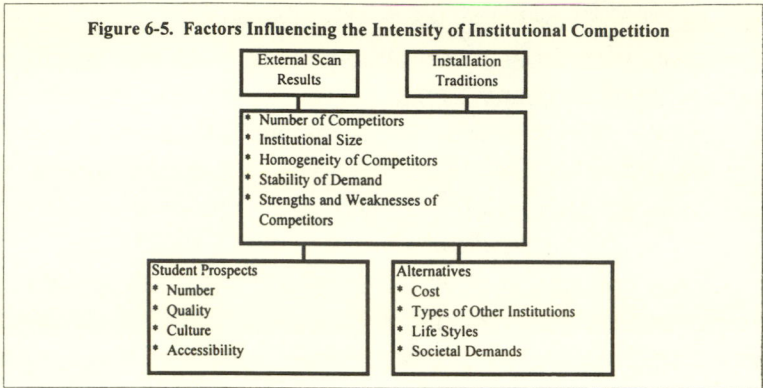

Figure 6-5. Factors Influencing the Intensity of Institutional Competition

Colleges, like individuals, have a difficult time growing beyond their roots. Small schools have been successful because they have been fulfilling a need in society. For them to transform themselves out of context with their historical roots is difficult and a questionable move. To drastically change their character may very well destroy the fabric of the institution. With respect to competitive analysis, however, a common problem appears to be that many colleges believe they know themselves well enough to survive in a discriminating market. In reality, their external image is quite different. Colleges need to continually refine their core image and not hold onto traditions which no longer serve them well in today's market. They need to better understand how they can compete in the educational marketplace without selling out their past.

During the growth years of higher education, worrying about selling out an institution's past was not a problem. The major problem was to keep up with the demand for higher education as shown in Table 6-2. During this growth period, small school planners would have been well served to be more sensitive to the impending infrastructure problems created by growing too quickly and beyond their ability to maintain a unique institutional character.

Table 6-2. The Growth of Higher Education in the United States

Year	Enrollment	Instit.	Studs/Inst
1950	2,296,592	1,859	1,235
1960	3,610,007	2,040	1,770
1970	8,649,368	2,573	3,361
1980	12,096,895	3,231	3,744
1989	13,043,118	3,535	3,690

Source: *1989-90 Fact Book on Higher Education*, United States. American Council on Education, 1989.

These planners would have also observed a normal marketplace phenomenon when demand outstrips supply. What occurs then is an increase in supply. In the United States, the number of institutions increased to meet the demand in student enrollments. It becomes apparent when reviewing these numbers that competition between colleges intensifies as student enrollments drop. In determining projected enrollment trends, Levine and Associates caution educators to make the distinction between college enrollment and college-going rate. They say that college enrollment is not merely a function of the number of births in a given year. They recommend the use of the external scan method to mitigate the college-going rate which will reflect the college enrollment.

Institutional size influences the intensity of competition due to the number of academic and extracurricular activities offered students. This is apparent in the flood of pamphlets and brochures prospective students receive as colleges try desperately to impress students with the range of programs that the institution offers. Competition becomes intense as each college rushes to keep pace.

Homogeneity has become a real concern for small private colleges. They have traditionally attracted a certain type of student. Given the costs of attendance, these students were typically the middle to upper-middle class.

Will the less economically advantaged groups of students, representing this country's primary minority populations, find the small school's historical character appealing? As small colleges try to understand how to attract more diverse students onto their campuses, they soon realize that homogeneity is a double-edge sword. As these institutions assess their own operations, they come to realize that their faculty, facilities, and lifestyle on campus have been historically conditioned to a homogeneous population. Attracting a more diverse student body to one's campus is only one aspect of the challenge. To change the faculty, staff, and administration's operating norms to deal with a diverse student body is another. Too many institutions are fixed by the history and the constraints of their routine operating norms. Furthermore, the way they react to the challenges of their competitor colleges and the changing prospective student population is limited by the constraints of their own internal perceptions.

In Summary

American educators, since colonial times, have been struggling to maintain their primacy over the classroom. The literature is filled with cases like the Dartmouth College court case of 1819, where a school was determined to maintain its independence.[20] However, even though educators may win their fair share of legal bouts in the courtrooms of America, the battle in the marketplace is another matter.

Colleges are quickly learning to listen to the pulse beat of society in order to maintain their foothold in the future. Faculty and administrators need to sort out where their institution is headed and start planning to revamp the infrastructure to make it happen. Many have heralded the use of Total Quality Management, TQM, as the cure-all for higher education. James L. Fisher, in his critique of the use of TQM for higher education, has sent up warning flares. Although there has been some success in the use of TQM in the profit sector, the endless use of graphs and charts without a focus wastes time and the goodwill of the faculty and staff. Fisher remarks that "...if TQM makes any sense at all in higher education, the key will be to adapt TQM in an environment specially emphasizing inspirational leadership, a long-range plan emphasizing where the institution wants to go (and how soon), individual accountability, and cost reduction."[21]

With Fisher's warning noted, small schools need to find a balance between the patterns of problem-blindness recognized by Nutt and Backoff, and a strict, robot-like adherence to programs like TQM.[22] Many schools, including some profiled in earlier chapters, have been to the brink of disaster and are fighting back to a very competitive position in their niche. Small schools have to find that niche and continue to stay abreast of the external movements in society.

CHAPTER VII
INTERNAL ENVIRONMENT:
ORGANIZATIONAL CHALLENGES

Stakeholders

The Demands on Colleges

The message from a small school president who recently led his institution through organizational change was clear and emphatic. Change is difficult, as it requires the organization to break routines which everyone has become comfortable and secure with over a long period of time. He related that everyone in the organization recognized that change was needed to survive, yet the resistance was staggering. The common cry was that change is fine, as long as it doesn't affect me. As this particular college president found out, efforts to introduce systemwide change can lead to a death struggle. What dies is the comfort zone that people work themselves into when a part of any organization.

Organizational behavioralists have provided many theories as to why people in organizations resist change. The risk of entering a situation which threatens to force people into changing behaviors and possibly losing power in the organization often creates an overwhelming anxiety and a need to protect oneself. To overcome this inherent resistance to organizational change, all constituencies must first understand those internal factors which are likely to be affected by the change process and how best to deal with them.

As stated in earlier chapters, small schools primarily sprang from the needs of a pluralistic society and their historical roots are deep. However, the complexities of modern society have placed a greater burden on these schools and all of higher education to adapt and change with the times. According to Larry Leslie and Paul Brinkman, today, colleges are asked to achieve seven roles for society. These goals are:

(1) Generate and disseminate knowledge.
(2) Stimulate learning in society.
(3) Educate the citizenry.
(4) Achieve specific educational objectives of society.
(5) Train the workforce.
(6) Enhance the economic growth and productivity of society.
(7) Provide equality of opportunity for society.[1]

Such demands can be extraordinarily complex for any institution to meet, yet implications of not responding to the expectations of those you serve is hardly an option for the modern school. These demands are not purely based on the market forces which influence the behavior of all colleges and universities. They are issues of accountability to a society which has high expectations of higher education.

The push for accountability in higher education has further led to a heightened awareness that institutions must be capable of accurately assessing themselves in order to make the best possible decisions. Institutional assessments have taken on ominous proportions in the past decade. The lack of well-developed and universally accepted models for institutional assessment has also resulted in a subtle yet real resistance to this important element of the decision-making process.

The 1988 General Secretary of the American Association of University Professors (AAUP), in frustration over assessment, commented that:

> The support of [assessment for accountability] by academic administrators is one more step in their metamorphosis from stewards to managers. The consequent diminution of the faculty's opportunity to exercise professional judgment would be one more step in their metamorphosis from professor to teaching assistant.[2]

In a more balanced view of the dilemma between professional autonomy desired by the faculty and accountability demanded by society, Derek Bok offers this view:

> it is inappropriate and unrealistic to expect professors to subordinate everything to helping students achieve a set of shared objectives. But it is equally wrong for faculties to pay no attention to common goals and to ignore the question of how well these aims are being realized.[3]

Bok appears to understand the dilemma---yet even we are given no answers on how to reconcile the expectations of some individuals with those of the organization. In fact, there can only be one answer if an institution is genuinely committed to the advancement of the organization. No academic institution will survive, let alone thrive, if it ignores the concerns of its primary provider, the faculty. Likewise, leadership can not abdicate their responsibility in assuring that all constituencies and legitimate stakeholders in the institution are also taken into consideration. There is no absolute authority in an academic organization, as all colleges and universities have historically and will likely continue to rely on the collective voice of stakeholders.

The Meaning of Stakeholders

Basically, stakeholders include all the groups who can significantly affect or be affected by an organization's decisions, policies, and operations.[4] In higher education, the number of varying groups of stakeholders seem almost endless, particularly if we consider those external to the institution. However, the primary stakeholders are also the most obvious. They are the internal groups that are most directly affected by the day-to-day activity of the institution--namely, students, professors, administrators, and the support staff. Much has been written about the interaction between these groups of stakeholders as they struggle to accomplish their respective agendas. The purpose of this discussion is to gain an understanding of the effect each group may have on institutional decision-making and, thus, the change effort at small schools.

The struggle to weight the decision making towards one's own interests often starts with the agenda setting process. Michael Parenti, in understanding the position of the powerless, made the observation that, "One of the most important aspects of power...is not [whether one] prevail[s] in a struggle but to predetermine the agenda of the struggle to determine whether certain questions ever reach the competition stage."[5]

When superimposing Parenti's view on an academic organization, it is not difficult to envision this scenario being played out in the many committees that are common to institutions of higher education. Essentially, each group, and usually each committee member, is vying to influence the decision-making of the committee and ultimately the institution toward their respective comfort zone.

An example of this would be an English professor, an expert in Elizabethan literature, sitting on a curriculum committee, deciding on the merit of adding a chemistry course to the university core requirement. On the surface, one would agree that a liberal arts education would require an appreciation of the scientific method of reasoning. Yet, under further scrutiny, the question becomes whether this addition to the core curriculum will affect the number of students who will take Elizabethan literature.

What the faculty member is faced with is a decision to balance the stake s/he has in this issue against that of others in the organization. When viewed from this perspective, it becomes quite clear that generally a check and balance is needed to sort out the tendency of most committee members to lobby for their own causes (agendas). It has long been understood that administrators responsible for select disciplinary areas are expected to protect the interest of that level of the hierarchy. The president, of course, is charged to do what is best for the institution as a whole. Presidents, however, also have the added responsibility of remaining sensitive to the needs of external stakeholders. For the modern college, these groups, in effect, become the invisible hand of the marketplace which cannot be ignored.

These secondary stakeholders include alumni, local businesses that depend on the income generated from the college's activities, regional and national businesses that are the future employers of the college's graduates, and, of course, government and society as a whole. Even if it is difficult to obtain an accurate pulse of the needs of these stakeholders, colleges must attempt to gather information that will provide the necessary insights as to their short and, more importantly, long-term needs.

To achieve the necessary direct contact with their alumni and local employers, many small colleges ask prominent businessmen, alumni, and educators to sit on their boards. They also have formed alumni boards and advisory committees consisting of local businessmen and educators. All this is a step in the right direction, however, a common problem is that people are asked to sit on these boards and committees because of their donation capability and prominence, not for their ability to help the college bridge the worlds of higher education and society.

As a result of this propensity to fill the board and committees with well-to-do individuals, the influence on the institution's operations, in regard to regional and national interests, is usually left up to Adam Smith's invisible hand. Reaction of the marketplace to the quality of the graduates, no matter how abhorrent the thought is to the faculty, is eventually felt in the long run. As will be discussed later in this chapter, a sense of false security normally prevails when no immediate danger exists to an organization; thus, administrators and faculty are often distant and maybe even oblivious as to the long-term effects of market conditions.

Colleges must be cautious not to bend to every whim of society. Yet, in the college's efforts to balance the demands of its stakeholders, there needs to be an informative appreciation of where society is moving and how institutions of higher education aid in this movement.

Coming full cycle on the question of the collegiate role, the seven goals of Leslie and Brinkman become even more significant when you weigh in the stakeholders of each of those goals and the problems involved with balancing their respective agendas in the operations of colleges. When analyzing goals four through seven, which involve achieving special educational objectives of society, educating the workforce, assisting in the economic growth and equal opportunity for members of society, it makes good sense for the financiers of higher education to hold administrators of higher education accountable for the resources given to them.

Unfortunately, this is not the operational scenario desired by most faculty and probably many administrators. Hazard Adams, in his satirical look at academic politics, lays the foundation for the differences between the faculty and administrators, and the myth that faculty long for the times when universities were "...truly collegial and all administrator's chores came about as a result of a division of responsibilities among faculty members,"[6] and not bounded by the rationality of financiers and the marketplace.

Referring to the other goals for higher education provided by Leslie and Brinkman, the faculty would probably accept and acknowledge the legitimacy of the first and second. However, even these academically-oriented goals have problems when questions such as how research projects are funded and what internal academic agendas are prefixed by constraints of money, academic structure, and politics.

When challenged, faculty and administrators would probably agree on Leslie and Brinkman's goals. However, when the list turns into a plan that attempts to rationally weigh the arguments and agendas of the various stakeholders, resistance can occur.

Change

The Process of Change

A candidate for the presidency of a small liberal arts college in North Carolina was asked by the search committee if he had any questions for them. He said he only had one. A little shocked by the mere fact that he had only one question, they were even more startled by the question. Before stating the question, he pointed out that they appeared to desperately need to change the way they had been operating. They realized that business as usual had put them on the brink of very difficult times and future prospects were not good. He took their silence as an admission of agreement and proceeded with his question. He said, "I sense your urgency to change the way things have been in the past, yet I wonder whether the board, administration and the faculty have the stomach for change."

In a very short statement, this candidate avowed the difficulty in changing the operating norms of a community and asked the board if they really were ready to meet the challenge. Although many jokes and ill feelings are laid at the feet of Machiavelli for his book *The Prince*, Machiavelli can be credited with formalizing the difficulty any organization has with the change process. Although no one advocates the demise of incumbents, it is common for presidents of both, colleges and industry, to bring in or choose their own team--a twentieth-century solution for the Prince.

No doubt there are many examples of organizations that overcome their lack of orderly transition to the future through (1) the sheer force of the uniqueness of their products or services, (2) the restriction of competition through governmental protection such as laws and tariffs, and (3) the scarcity of the product or service being offered. In the long run, however, failure to recognize and manage those internal factors which affect an institution's well-being will eventually weaken its viability.

The mere thought of linking institutional operations to market-driven forces can be a bitter reality for some and not readily accepted. As stated earlier, we saw this reaction even from at least one small school president. Consequently, it is no wonder the planning process has been one of continual struggle for small schools. Faculty, as attested to by the presidents interviewed for this book, see the planning process as a struggle to retain their power over the educational process or, at the very least, to control the direction of curricular and faculty development. Administrators see the planning process as a necessary evil which is needed to focus the energies of the community. As discussed in the previous section, the conflict between faculty and administrators results from competing demands of internal and external stakeholders. Thus, faculty are left with the fear that curricular development will be a product of supply and demand curves, the fluctuation of interest rates and marketing gimmickry to attract students.

This resistance to a separation between external forces and the internal operations of the campus is not new to American colleges. Administrators and faculty have historically felt the need to collegially control the educational process. Hence, the need to administer to the needs of faculty and students has been the preferred method of control, rather than managing the educational process with all its business-like implications.

Murphy, in reviewing the universality of the management concept, stated that management is an organizational concept, not merely a business concept.[7] To many individuals, especially those in academe, the concepts of management and business only reflect a profit orientation. Not surprisingly then, planning, organizing, motivating, and controlling, all functions of management, can send academicians into a frenzy of mistrust and an uncompromising position when it comes to working with administrators to help maintain their viability.

In analyzing the trend of how colleges were administered over the past three decades, it is apparent that they have begun to sound and act more and more like the profited-oriented corporations that they have come to disdain.[8] Competing with one another for the best reputation, for the best professors, for the best students and, now, for the best bargain for the price, all are symptomatic of organizations trying to maintain their vitality in the marketplace.

In a historical perspective, Lawrence Veysey tells us that this competitive struggle for reputation and resources is not new to academe. He goes so far as to say that the struggle for a reputation by colleges during the 1700s and 1800s had important consequences in the development of colleges. To gain respectability during that time period, he stated that American colleges were credited with fostering more innovation and fluidity in their academic development than their European counterparts.[9] Paradoxically, even though the American college maintained its competitive edge with its European counterparts through the years, the verve for change has somehow been lost in many of today's academic institutions.

In studying the developments of today's high-technology businesses, one can glean lessons from firms that try to survive by operating on the cutting edge of their industry. Hearing such terminology linked to education at first seems strange. Yet, at the American Association for Higher Education (AAHE) Conference held in April 1992, Henry Cisneros, a former mayor of San Antonio, echoed this call to the American higher education system. At the conference, Cisneros stated that higher education needs to be on the "cutting edge" of a rapidly transforming society. If he is right, then institutions can no longer operate as they have in the past--entrenched in the mentality that higher education is immune to the market forces that challenge all other institutions.

To maintain viability on the cutting edge of educational developments, academicians need to understand organizations as an interrelated system of parts. Ludwig von Bertalanffy tells us that organizations are like living organisms that need to have their health checked regularly in order for them to maintain their focus and direction. He thought that it was possible to develop a systematic framework for describing relationships that occur in organizations, and thus provide managers a framework from which to guide the organization. In sum, he envisioned the organization as a system of interrelated parts that closely resembled the functioning of any living organism.[10] Using this concept of an organizational system, we can start to analyze the different components of an organization such as a college.

Normally, when one thinks of an organizational structure, the bureaucratic model quickly comes to mind. Rules, regulations, and tight supervisory control are usually expressed in the same breath. These characteristics, unfortunately, conjure images of lost freedom and creativity, especially to the academicians who need their academic freedom to maintain the vitality of their respective disciplines.

The bureaucratic design, as many students of organizational studies come to appreciate, sprang from the era in our history when the Industrial Revolution was forcing humanity to redesign the workplace. Working conditions in the emerging new workplace required a more controlled environment if any semblance of timeliness and order was to be obtained. This new workplace called for the massing of large workforces in order to achieve the economies of scale desired in an industrialized setting.[11]

Without going into depth on the pros and cons of bureaucratic structures as shown in Figure 7-1, it should be realized that there is a continuum of designs that administrators may use to divide the task and responsibilities in their institutions. The problem for administrators is to find that structure (design) which best fits the institution's mission, external and internal environment, and its people. In addressing this problem educators seem to have an all-or-nothing mentality. As depicted in Figure 7-1, this all-or-nothing approach is reflected by either one extreme of the continuum (the bureaucratic design), or the other extreme (totally organic, which embraces the philosophy of free-flowing relationships and very little constraints to operating procedures).

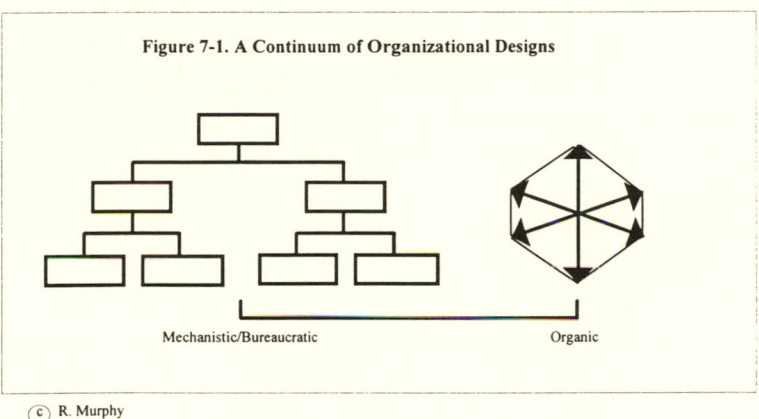

Figure 7-1. A Continuum of Organizational Designs

Mechanistic/Bureaucratic   Organic

ⓒ R. Murphy

As administrators in small schools search for the configuration that will best suit their institution, there should be an understanding that congruity needs to exist between structure, task, and the internal and external environments of organizations. In attempting to achieve this balance, all too often the complexity of the task overrides the effort that is needed to refine the proper structure and working relationships, thus, the extremes of the continuum too often become the solution. However, in the change process, each of these factors is extremely critical if any organization is expected to evolve to the viable form of existence that is desired.

Business and industry have seen this continuum of organizational structures becoming more complex with the movement toward modular organizational designs. In these designs, permanent relationships within an organization become obsolete. The thrust is to have a core unit which will be the focus for building the remainder of the organization. The relationships between the core unit and other external agencies are temporary in nature and last as long as the market requires this association. The watchword here is extreme flexibility.

Educators may disassociate the use of this organizational design technique, yet, we can see it already in not-for-profit operations like hospitals and educational institutions. Hospitals can no longer afford to exist in a community and compete with a sister hospital. Either a permanent merger or an arrangement occurs where certain services are conducted at the respective hospital, clinic, or infirmary. Small schools have already moved in this direction through joint agreements with high schools, community colleges, and sister institutions that share specific expertises or facilities in order to save the expense of duplicating a costly operation or a scarce resource.

Critics have come forth to warn about the lack of loyalty and chaotic existence that may result in such relationships. To develop the comraderie which is often necessary in order to attain a mature, closely-knit organization requires continual contact and an interdependence in the daily routines of the institution. Farming out various operations, it is felt, will lessen the opportunity for the various parts of the institution to become integrated. In small schools where one of their trademarks is a communal environment, this modualization of the classroom may be a major obstacle.

On the other hand, if von Bertalanffy is right about organizations being living, open-ended systems, small schools, like hospitals, must share their resources with sister instititutions or feel the burden of too few patrons for their services. Many educators would rather not face this dilemma. As much as this idyllic state may be desired, society can not foot the bill, thus, organizations must adapt in order to survive.

A very important concept that needs to be addressed in understanding the survival strategies of organizations is the realization that all organizations, whether bureaucratic or organic, are forced relationships. These forced relationships, under the continuous threat of breaking down, must be continuously nurtured, culled, and pruned in order to maintain the health and currency of these relationships. If not, these relationships, as well as the entire organization, will move toward an entropic state. With this understanding of the entropic tendencies of organizations, the need for plans, policies, procedures, and assessment becomes obvious. Once this is understood, it is not a difficult leap to understand that the tasks, structure, and power relationships within organizations are all, or should be, a function of (1) the overall purpose of the organization, (2) the pressures applied to the organization by external agencies, and (3) the strengths and weaknesses of the organization's internal assets to achieve its purpose. As seen in the previous section, this is usually very difficult, given the sheer number of agendas presented by the many stakeholders of the institution.

Notwithstanding this challenge, administrators of small colleges are striving to balance these three functions while trying to assist each stakeholder entity to achieve its intended purpose. Without some structure to focus the energies of the individuals within the organization, intended purpose easily becomes the optimal condition for each entity within the institution. James March and Herbert Simon in their classical text, *Organizations,* discussed this issue under the concept of bifurcation of interests.[12] In today's terminology, we use the word suboptimization, the state where entities within an organization move to optimize their own conditions. Unfortunately, it is usually at the expense of other entities in the organization. In order to prevent the suboptimizing of the overall good of the institution, plans, procedures, policies, and leadership need to be focused on maintaining the focus of the organization and the relationships within.

A corollary effect on suboptimization is displacement of objectives. As organizations strive to evolve to more suitable forms of existence, the interest of stakeholders moves to replace the goals of the institution. Put another way, the means by which elements within the organization help achieve the institution's goals eventually become an end unto themselves. In institutions of higher education with diverse agendas and stakeholders, agreement must be reached as to the goals at each level and how to achieve them. This is the purpose of the planning process and the subsequent plan. Plans must include goals and objectives and how to assess the accomplishment of each. If not, intended purpose becomes defined by each stakeholder individually.

Assessment has been a thorn in the side of academe for many years. Many academics will say that assessment stifles the freedom of the faculty. Others who are fighting for accountability of the societal resources given to educational institutions demand a strict system of assessment. More importantly, assessment is merely a system of appraising the status and progress of an institution's efforts to accomplish its goals and objectives. In essence, this system should be designed to represent fixed reference points by which to measure progress toward a desired outcome. In a planning guide for independent schools, Susan Stone rebuffs this concern by stating that planning and assessment of one's status is needed for one reason, survival. She continues by saying:

> with issues such as changing family structures and social values, an unsettled economy, shifts in demographics--particularly among the school-age population, advances in all areas of technology, retraining for multi-career lives, and the shifting profile of who will be teaching in independent schools...considering any one of these factors could be the catalyst for change, can independent schools afford not to plan ahead?[13]

The process of change is likened to the proverbial tar baby. Once you grab on and attempt to make the necessary modifications needed in the institution, be it in structure, people process, or facilities, the ripple effect throughout the organization seems endless. Controlling the effects is the tar baby syndrome. Administrators in small schools attempt to balance the agendas of each stakeholder. Yet once they get immersed into the issues of the stakeholders, it's hard to extract themselves from the struggle by trying to gracefully put the issue in its proper perspective, and thus, to rest.

Creating Change in Higher Education

To employ a cliche, change is inevitable. A corollary, of course, is that not to try to manage one's destiny is foolhardy. As previously suggested, to prevent entropy from occurring, college administrators must find the balance between their rich academic heritage and the type of operations required to face the demands of a marketplace that forces them to be effective, efficient, and responsive to the needs of society. Robert Newton uses the symbolism of the two cultures of Academe to portray the continuing conflict between the "...corporation, or organized, business-like body or guild, and the very personal, sometimes contentious community of teachers and learners."[14] As this scenario is played out between these two cultures, a move toward a cohesive institutional purpose becomes difficult.

Studies show that as organizations change to meet the challenges of their environments, the most successful ones are those that recognize the factors affecting their development and adjust appropriately. Philip Sadler considers Western society to be undergoing rapid change and radical transformation and states, "...it follows that institutions and organizations which survive and prosper will be those most capable of adapting to a changed world."[15] Relating this observation to academe, A. Yudof, dean of the school of law at the University of Texas at Austin, remarked that "universities must make hard decisions about institutional priorities instead of unrealistically attempting to be world class in every discipline."[16]

Major challenges are facing today's institutions of higher education. As campus leaders decide how best to address these challenges, faculty have become worried whether their views will help frame solutions. As an example, a common challenge today is the extent to which colleges get involved in internationalization. Maurice Harrai notes that the need to internationalize higher education is recognized by most institutions. However, he remarks that "... on too many of our campuses efforts to internationalize the curriculum, to implement study abroad, or to take advantage of the presence of international students...do not connect with each other."[17] The pressure for change in higher education seems to be on the minds of most educators.

According to Russell Rogers, higher education, in particular, must face difficult challenges in order to change its operating environment.[18] Oversized budgets, fixed facility costs, and changing student populations have caused higher education to reevaluate the way it operates. As can be expected, various stakeholders in higher education are vying for power to control the direction of colleges and universities. To the distress of the faculty, these external influences manifest themselves through power-setting agendas, generated within various committees throughout the campus. It also reflects, they feel, a move toward monetary efficiency that comes into direct conflict with the traditional intellectual roots of a university, namely, the search for and dissemination of knowledge.

Donald Norris and Nick Poulton, in a primer for new university planners, provide a helpful synopsis of the evolution of university planning. In their synopsis, they showed that prior to the 1940s there was little need for colleges to operate as market-oriented institutions.[19] As the doors opened for the masses to enter higher education, the increase in number of institutions and subsequent faculty was inevitable. Between 1950 and 1970, institutions of higher education increased from 1,859 institutions to 2,573, a rise of 38 percent. As of 1994, 3,638 institutions are in existence, an increase of 41 percent since 1970 and 96 percent since 1950. Enrollment during the 1950 to 1970 time period increased by 273 percent. Projections between 1950 and 1995 show that enrollment will have increased by 367 percent, or 12.5 million students.[20]

William Massy speculates that the *massification* of higher education changed the operations of institutions drastically. He postulates that three significant developments evolved to counteract the effects of massification: (1) academic institutions grew so large that states became compelled to track the use of public funds, (2) hand in hand with fiscal accountability was the public cry for more specific criteria to evaluate educational services rendered, and, lastly, (3) there was a need to closely link an institution's revenues to market variables.[21]

This shift to educate the masses is seen as a result of societal pressures for more equitable social justice. Some in academe fear that this movement to widen the doors of colleges was at the expense of quality. They revised their estimate as institutions moved to improve their educational programs. They contend that this was a result of the pressure mounted by external stakeholders for colleges to be accountable for the high cost of tuition and the access they are allowed to society's prospective students.[22] From a market point of view, one might contend that this move toward quality reflects the basic instinct of any organization to distinguish its services from competitors and not just a reaction to the pressures of external stakeholders. In reality, it is probably a combination of both.

As economic factors continue to impinge on institutions of higher education, faculty are concerned that monetary, rather than intellectual agendas, will become the primary concern of their institutions. Faculty ask, How can we meaningfully generate and evaluate appropriate agendas and weigh the decisions that may critically affect our academic life? Although most faculty dislike the term management connected to the education process, Boyer contends that faculty see their presidents in this role.[23] University administrators, conversely, are becoming more aware that they must be proactive in the development of their institution. The traditional role of the passive facilitator will no longer suffice.

Planning for Change

Strategic decision-making emerged as a viable practice for business and industry planning in the late 1970s and early 1980s.[24] Much was written in the first few years of the 1980s about the subject, although there is not overwhelming evidence of any significant implementation of this management practice by colleges and universities.[25]

Strategic decision-making as an operational concept for academia was and still is in its infancy. After two hundred years of relative strength through continued growth and expansion, higher education found itself in the 1970s coping with a very uncertain future. This situation was created by the combined effects of economic, demographic, and political forces taking shape in the United States. The new management vocabulary for leadership now includes retrenchment, stringency, uncertainty, reduction, and decline.[26]

By the end of the 1970s, higher education was searching for new models to map its future and survive a crisis decision-making mentality. Colleges soon discovered that they could not simply transplant strategic planning models designed for business and industry into their unique organizational environments. Frequently, rational models of decision-making are rejected in an academic environment. This results from the presumption that academic environments, by their very nature, are not conducive to highly structured and hierarchical decision paths.

Throughout the 1980s, the principles of strategic planning slowly gained recognition in higher education. The potential stumbling blocks to more timely and effective planning in higher education included (1) complicated and time-consuming process, (2) the gap between planners and doers in the organization, (3) frequent leadership turnover, (4) budgets poorly linked to planning, (5) plans that never materialized, and, finally, (6) leadership is too often consumed in crisis management to develop long-term perspectives.[27] These, and other issues, such as diversity, quality, and rising costs, are forcing colleges to embrace the idea of strategic decision-making.

Visionaries such as George Keller emerged as disciples for academic strategic decision-making and provided the educational community with a model for self-analysis. Keller's agenda for change includes acknowledgement by the higher education community that survival beyond the 1980s means coming to terms with social conditions such as a free-market driven economy and competitive positioning. As a central theme, he suggests that traditional posturing of administrative versus faculty prerogatives will not ultimately support and sustain a school which is struggling to remain competitive.[28] Rather, academic leadership must recognize that determining the strategic direction of the modern college or university and producing positive change requires the enlistment of all parties with an investment in the enterprise.

Responding to the uncertainties of the times, Keller echoes the need for strategic decision-making in an academic environment and perhaps, more importantly, the necessity of full community involvement in the process. This position was a radical departure from the rational scientific models of strategic planning employed in American business and industry.

For much of the past decade, the debate has not centered on whether colleges should be, or are capable of, engaging in a strategic planning process. It is generally accepted that as a dynamic enterprise, such activity is not only desirable but essential for a college.

As colleges and universities have become increasingly market driven, academic leadership has sought out and incorporated strategic planning, particularly as a function of enrollment planning initiatives. Strategic marketing, popularized by Philip Kotler and Karen Fox in the mid-1980s, provides another model for institutional planning. Their focus is on developing a comprehensive approach to assessing the competitive position of the organization.[29] A growing number of schools are analyzing their environment, markets and competition, assessing their strengths and weaknesses, and developing a clear sense of mission, target market, and market positioning.

Since no truly standard academic model exists for the academic planning process, only adaptations of business and industry practices, the role of the faculty has been a hotly debated topic. This challenge recognized by researchers of higher education organization and governance in the early 1980s, still exists today. James Miller from the University of Michigan said:

> On the substantive front it appears that elements which will make up the new theory will include a strong emphasis on leadership and centralization. However, the relative emphasis which will be placed upon leadership through control and leadership through influence is unclear. In practice there is an increase in centralized control, which contrasts with the fact that in the most widely read literature, the emphasis is on some version of leadership through influence.[30]

Ellen Chaffee (1984) studied the financial difficulties of troubled small, private colleges where she examined the merits of two approaches to strategic management which are fundamentally different yet ultimately proved to be interdependent. This seminal study provides current researchers of faculty participation in strategic decision-making a framework for analyzing the critical relationship between individuals and their organizational unit.[31]

The adaptive model suggests the organization, as an integrated unit, should be sensitive and responsive to the needs of the changing marketplace. The interpretive model suggests that the organization is a network of self-interested participants, all of whom have consented to act together as long as their individual interests are satisfied. One of the most significant findings of this study is that the apparent conflict of these two models can be resolved when leadership is cognizant of the needs of individuals as well as the total organization. The study concluded that the most successful formula for carrying out strategic management initiatives in these small schools would combine the two models and further--if the two approaches to strategy suggest conflicting courses of action--the interpretive strategy should take precedence.

Leadership

What Is Leadership?

The eternal question to be answered in regard to leadership is, "If no one follows, does one lead?" Although there are many who discount the semantic differences between leading, managing, and administering, the distinctions are significant when trying to move an organization toward its mission. Stephen Robbins defines leadership as the ability to influence a group toward the achievement of goals.[32] Gregory Moorhead and Ricky Griffin add to this definition the qualifier that influence has to be of a non-coercive nature.[33] In his handbook on leadership, Ralph Stogdill lays out eleven variations of the concept based on whether one considers the focus to be a process, behavior, or an art form.[34] The argument continues today as to what really is leadership and how can organizations either instill it in their managers or identify it in prospective managers or administrators.

The concept of manager is a little more fixed than that of leader. When analyzed in depth, however, it too becomes a very elusive concept. John Schermerhorn defines manager as a person who is responsible for the work performance of others. He also defines administrator as a manager in a public or nonprofit organization as opposed to a business concern.[35] In other words, these definitions are based on legitimate power such as formal authority. As long as administrators are duly appointed in authority over others, they have become managers.

Leadership also has a limitation, namely, the appearance of influencing the behavior of others. If the desires of the leader are accomplished by the individual(s), then the leader usually gets credit for being effective, regardless of whether or not you use the non-coercive qualifier in your definition of leader. Given these limitations, a question arises when individuals accomplish the desired goal of the organization in spite of the influence used by the leader. Is this bad leadership? In fact, we know there are other explanations which could account for the goal achievement by individuals within an organization.

Systems View of Leadership

Utilizing the theoretical prism of von Bertalanffy's systems approach to analyze organizations, the influence process in groups can be considered. Without going into the myriad of leadership and motivational theories in the literature, a general appreciation can be honed with a systems view of leadership. In Figure 7-2, the use of a Venn diagram aids in understanding the relationship between four major factors that affect the behavior of individuals in an organization. U represents all the actions that are possible in an organization by an individual or a group. A represents those action that are influenced by a leader, while B represents those actions elicited from individuals as a result of the context and content of the work situation; for example, structure, working conditions, and tasks. The value system and all the other personal characteristics that make people who they are, are represented by the circle labeled C. Framed in this way, we can see that very few actions are strictly the result of a leader's influence. People may be reacting to the leader in the desired way but for different motivations. Additionally, the size and shape of each of these major factors are not fixed. They are different for each organization.

When viewed in this light, leadership in organizations, and in higher education, needs to be reexamined to gain new perspectives on this process, and more importantly, to glean a better understanding of how organizational components interact with each other. As plans, policies, and procedures are developed, a better understanding of the theoretical underpinnings of an organization will permit a more realistic understanding of the life of the organization.

A leadership technique used in organizations to gain more active involvement by individuals is participative management. This allows leaders/managers/administrators to actively include individuals within the organization into

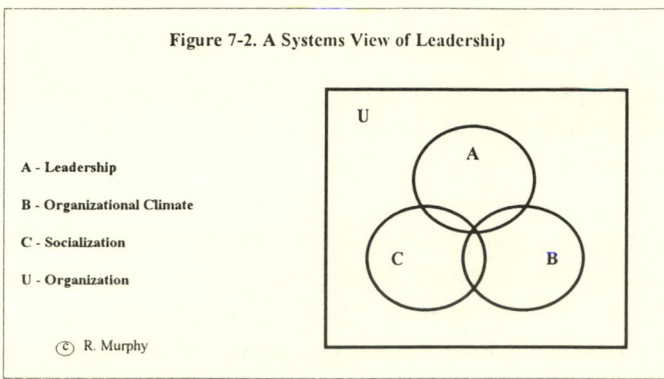

Figure 7-2. A Systems View of Leadership

A - Leadership

B - Organizational Climate

C - Socialization

U - Organization

ⓒ R. Murphy

the decision-making process. Although this technique is quite common in organizations and in higher education in faculty senates and college committees, there are certain problems with this approach.

Collective Leadership

We have seen the ideology of collective leadership develop in the literature through studies of participatory management. It is an ideology based upon a set of assumptions that suggest an individual, under certain conditions, will willingly and vigorously work to advance the goals of the organization through participation in a collective effort with other similarly motivated individuals. Over the past century, this theory has evolved from the classical and scientific models of organizational management and an emphasis on a controlled environment to a more modern and enlightened view of the individual contributing employee. Central to this view is the idea that management can encourage and support interaction among all potential contributors, creating a sense of ownership in the enterprise, resulting in positive change for the organization as an integrated unit.

Douglas McGregor is credited with shaping modern theories of participatory management. Influenced by earlier psychological work in self-actualization and modern views of power and values in the workplace, McGregor established guiding principles which continue to have a profound impact on the changing nature of organizational management.[36] These principles can be found in virtually all current literature on participatory management and include:

- Active participation by all involved.
- A transcending concern with individual dignity, worth, and growth.
- Re-examination and resolution of the conflict between individual needs and organizational goals through effective interpersonal relationships between superiors and subordinates.
- A concept of influence that relies not on coercion, compromise, evasion or avoidance, pseudosupport or bargaining, but on openness, confrontation, and working through differences.
- A belief that human growth is self-generated and furthered by an environment of trust, feedback, and authentic human relationships.

Analysis of McGregor's work gives us an insight as to the human disposition to work. Basically, he contends that if men dislike work and use it merely to provide food, shelter, and clothing, then a stern hand may be needed to accomplish organizational goals. He called this the Theory

X perspective. His Theory Y takes a more idyllic look at man. From this perspective, the worker is seen as internally motivated and seeks added responsibilities and a sense of accomplishment at work. An extension of McGregor's work was provided by Willard Zangwill, with later interpretation of William Ouchi in their Theory Z model. In the model, Theory Z takes a systemic approach to the integration of individual and organizational goals. It includes a series of actions which management must pursue in order to reinforce behavior, including goal setting, reinforcement, feedback, and error correction.[37]

From an ideological perspective, Theory Z differs from the Theory Y model only in the employment of external controls to assure a sense of order in the total organization. At issue is the degree of controls which any organization must have in place to avoid chaos while not inhibiting individual performance and contribution. This balanced perspective between meeting the motivational needs of individuals while effectively managing complex environments is probably closer to the reality of modern organizations.

In trying to apply these theories to academe, and more specifically, small schools, the question that must be addressed is, "How does one view the individuals within the institution." One must be careful to categorize any group of individuals within the college as either Theory X or Theory Y. The intent of McGregor was more in line with helping managers better understand the general motivational patterns in the workplace rather than trying to categorize certain groups of workers.

Ouchi's Theory Z is probably most applicable in small schools because it is based on the social organization and measures productivity in terms of individual contributions to the long-range vitality of the enterprise, which further complements the values of such institutions. According to Ouchi, there are three characteristics which a Theory Z organization will exhibit:

- Trust: There is a willingness to make sacrifices through the knowledge that such sacrifices will be equitably repaid in the future.
- Subtlety: There is an understanding that interpersonal relationships are complex and constantly changing, and management needs to be discerning and have the ability to make fine distinctions about these relationships.
- Intimacy: There is a need for caring, supportive, and unselfish behavior among organizational members, with a belief that close social relations are necessary.[38]

The ideology of participatory management and particularly the almost idealistic organizational view of Theory Z has been questioned in both industry and education. At the center of the debate are the cultural differences between Japanese and American organizations. Whereas Americans cherish their independence and sense of individuality, harmony is placed on an even higher pedestal in Japan. After Ouchi's work there was a minor flurry of criticism from the academic community with respect to applications of Theory Z within a college or university setting. This criticism is best captured in the following excerpt from a speech delivered at 1984 AAHE National Conference:

Decision making in Japanese universities is so

closely tied to the culture and its value system that it is difficult to perceive what Americans can borrow on a reasonable scale. Harmony has long been important in Japan and is used as a building block to develop the consensus approach in decision making--in addition, the individual is still the primary unit in our society and in our educational system, while the group welfare predominates in Japan.[39]

The Theory Z organization does set a high standard for consensus building, and this, perhaps more than any other dimension of the model, evokes the greatest criticism. Full consensus on major decision-making, particularly of a strategic nature, is perhaps an unrealistic expectation. However, there is virtually no disagreement with the underlying principles and intent of participatory models of organizational management. The ideology of participatory management has survived and even been resurrected through the currently popular total quality management movement (TQM).

This recent phenomenon in business and industry is yet another example of the tendency of organizations to eventually seek to maximize the potential of individual contributors. While relatively little research has actually been carried out in the application of total quality management principles in higher education, there is growing interest to do so from colleges and universities. Over the past several years, increasing numbers of colleges and universities have turned to TQM to reconsider institutional management.[40]

Through our systems of academic self-governance and

a fundamental commitment to collegiality, we embrace the ideology of participatory management, if not actually attempt to put it into practice. Jean Wyer wrote a piece comparing John Millet's collegial model to the then emerging Theory Z. In this comparative study, she describes the central themes of community and what she calls devotion to purpose as cornerstones of both models.[41] As stated above, intended purpose of any organization is at the mercy of interpretation by each stakeholder and stakeholder group. Care must be taken in embracing Wyer's proposition unless each group has accepted the operational definitions that make up the purpose of the organization.

Although the participatory model calls for shared responsibility in this new working relationship, it is generally agreed that the onus is on administration to take the first step. Administration is often closest and most sensitive to the external conditions which are most likely to influence major decisions affecting the campus. The age-old debate over faculty governance is now a much broader and more complex question, as mounting external pressures often pose a greater threat to the institution than internal relations.

Since the 1970s, we see less debate over which constituency on campus has a right to be involved in major decisions. Today, attention has shifted more to administration's responsibility to seek out and engage everyone with a vested interest in the outcome. This change has affected administration's working relationship with faculty senates, unions, and representative groups such as the AAUP. K. Mortimer and T.R. McConnell argued, however, that "the legitimacy and effectiveness of faculty senates are threatened by their unrepresentativeness and their inability to act quickly and decisively in times of crisis...and, faculty unions are often presented as an alternative or supplement to senates, but we see no evidence that they are any more representative of faculty than are senates."[42] The burden frequently rests with administration to identify and engage faculty who truly represent the interests of the larger constituency.

The Gordian Knot of Academic Leadership

Although we have focused primarily on the role of leadership in fostering a participatory environment, faculty also have a critical role to play. Due to the relatively recent interest in the participatory model, as applied to strategic planning and decision-making, there has not been a great deal written with respect to faculty responsibility. As early as 1971, institutional planners were challenging faculty and their representative bodies such as the AAUP to help shape the new definition of governance. Among the issues identified were:

- The attitudes and values of long-range planning and its function in colleges and universities, including a resistance on the part of faculty to change.
- Recognition of institutional planning as an important ancillary function of other existing faculty committees.
- The need to encourage faculty to be pro-active rather than reactive.[43]

Another obstacle to faculty involvement in planning and strategic decision-making is their general lack of expertise and the requisite reward systems to encourage them to take an active role in academic administration. Most faculty have not been trained, nor are they professionally motivated, to engage in strategic decision-making. This problem was identified and is mentioned in the literature as early as the late 1970s. Lloyd claimed, "Faculty are usually experts in their field which, with the exception of management related programs, seldom include planning. Moreover, the faculty are seldom substantially rewarded for developing expertise in planning and in developing and carrying out a plan."[44]

There is little evidence administration has taken any overt action to change this condition and some researchers, such as Chan believe that, "While there exists well-established mechanisms and approaches for faculty participation in areas traditionally reserved for faculty prerogatives, such as tenure, promotion, and curriculum, the literature on effective and desirable ways to involve faculty in strategic planning is still at the developmental stage."[45]

While we often take the more negative view that faculty are losing their voice in college decision-making, research is showing that this is not necessarily the case at all schools. A study conducted in the mid-1980s of 21 liberal arts colleges reported that 16 of them demonstrated a strengthened/expanded faculty role, 4 showed no change, and only 1 reported a diminished faculty role.[46]

A major project of the Association for the Study of Higher Education in 1985 concluded that the discussion and debate on faculty participation in institutional decision making will continue and has broad implications for future development of the literature and discovery of new theory. It called for the following from academic scholars:

- Refinement of the terminology...greater efforts to distinguish between participation, power, influence, and autonomy.
- Establishment of a rationale for faculty participation, including performance measurement, quality of work life, and job satisfaction.
- Development of faculty leadership.
- Organizational and political dynamics...a better understanding of patterns of conflict and consensus.
- Development of administrative leadership.[47]

In Summary

This chapter has portrayed the challenging conditions under which all internal stakeholders must function in the decision-making process of an institution. Regardless of size or character, these are the internal conditions which can be found on virtually any college campus and must be dealt with in the strategic process. Even small schools, like their larger counterparts, have multiple stakeholders, all of whom hold a vested interest in the welfare of the institution and an expectation to share in the decision-making process. It is an inherent characteristic of higher education and one which should be exploited, not denied.

In 1960, Douglas McGregor began a movement that has touched all organizations, in and outside of education, which are committed to the discovery of optimization of people. McGregor's desire to construct a theoretical framework in which to better understand the conditions under which this can be achieved was no doubt influenced by his professional experiences at Swarthmore and later presidency of Antioch College. It is perhaps not coincidental that these two small liberal arts colleges have indeed helped shape modern thinking on the theoretical foundations of participatory management.

CHAPTER VIII
NEW DIRECTIONS FOR
INSTITUTIONAL DECISION-MAKING

Organizational Context

Colleges and universities have traditionally striven to be and been treated as special institutions in our society. There is general agreement that the educational process often requires a structural looseness, precluding a fixation on coordinated processes and standardized outputs. An educational institution is also a dynamic environment with a synergy that is built upon the collective capacity, energy, and will of its many stakeholders. Yet, for all these conditions, colleges are realizing that regardless of whatever unique status each may desire or have, none is immune from today's market forces. These forces must be reckoned with within the context of the existing organization if the institution expects to survive.

Virtually all colleges and universities are competing for limited public support, even those within the private sector. Consequently, there is increasing public pressure to be efficient and effective organizations, capable of managing and capitalizing on limited resources. This has been a difficult challenge, as many institutions have not inculcated management practices for being either efficient or effective. Yet, there is evidence that a number of institutions, particularly in the small school sector, have both understood and met this challenge. It is from these exemplary practices that other institutions will learn and adapt to the inevitable forces of the marketplace.

The old cliche that the best-laid plan is only as good as the process and people to implement it is never more poignant than in an institution of higher education. Henry Mintzberg, in his effort to sensitize managers and administrators to the problems of using planning to create change, forewarns that "no amount of elaboration will ever enable formal procedures to forecast discontinuities, to inform managers [/administrators] who are detached from their operations, to create novel strategies."[1] He stresses that analysis will not serve as a substitute for a process of synthesis, one that understands the culture and realities of the organization. Even in his 1994 book, which strongly attacks formal strategic planning, Mintzberg does not suggest that analysis of external and internal environments isn't important, but rather that the resulting information needs to be placed in its proper context.[2] Such a context is one that understands the strengths and weaknesses of the organization and further allows the change process to include participation of major stakeholders.

To fully appreciate the strategic positioning of an academic institution, one point in particular must be re-emphasized as we close this story of small schools. Academic leaders must understand and appreciate the fact that an academic institution is largely dependent upon the effective ulitilization of the faculty, its primary resource. Therefore, it is administration's responsibility to capitalize on the individual as well as collective strength of this primary resource group. Through their control of the curriculum, political clout within the organization, and continual contact with students, faculty can make or break an institution's strategic initiative.

Mobilizing Faculty

This book has been about small schools, their early history, evolution as a community, and, at least for some, dramatic reversal in fortunes over the past twenty years. It has also examined the changing character of small schools struggling to remain competitive while preserving their rich heritage and unique place in higher education. In spite of predictions that small schools could not survive, institutions such as Keuka College have succeeded in remaining competitive. They have done so through innovative initiatives, effective management of institutional resources, and adaptation to external social and economic conditions. Aggressive leadership and equally important, the engagement of faculty in the strategic process, has led Keuka, as well as many of the other institutions profiled, to their current state of stability and competitive position in the marketplace.

This book has also provided an opportunity to examine the challenge of uniting two, still developing, ideas in higher education administration--the strategic decision process and principles of participatory management. The intrinsic value of having faculty committed to an institutional mission and common sense of purpose is immeasurable and an important message to all schools. In this regard, small schools are demonstrating an ability to survive by understanding their environment and involving primary stakeholder groups such as the faculty.

Although we speak of the ideology of community, a shared vision and a set of values which everyone in the organization believes in, it would be more appropriate and strategic to optimize this characteristic of small schools. As depicted in the various case studies, small schools possess unique organizational characteristics, often centered on the faculty, which can be used as a distinct strategic advantage in the marketplace. It is the responsibility of academic leaders to recognize this potential and exploit it in the most positive sense.

This book has illustrated that the character of small schools was continuously redefined as new variables were introduced throughout the evolution of higher education in the United States. These included the social and economic conditions of the country, enrollment fluctuations of the student body, demands on leadership, and, most importantly, the changing expectations for faculty. Each era in the development of small schools has had implications on the working relationship of faculty and administration. We can return to the previously detailed experiences of Keuka College and examine just a few of these changes as this institution embodies the challenges and conquests of small schools over the past one hundred years.

A Legacy of Patriarchal Leadership

From 1890, until the departure of Dr. Norton in the mid-1930s, the strong, intensive, and patriarchal style of Keuka's leadership clearly dominated institutional decision-making. This leadership style was indicative of the times and could be found throughout the fledging small-school sector. These were not merely presidents; they were the creators of this country's small schools, whose names are synonymous with the institutions themselves. Their legacies live on today in the strength of character and resilency of the institution.

Through the vision of these early leaders in small schools, the college would become the focal point of the surrounding community. This is still the case today as many small schools play a central role in the health and welfare of the greater community. History reflects that some of these early leaders, such as those at Keuka College, did not allow their church sponsorship to distract them from a secular vision of education. Consequently, these early leaders often took bold and innovative steps to competitively position their institutions.

By the early 1900s, many of these institutions were beginning a slow but gradual separation from church control. A new generation of leaders in small schools at the turn of the century would be guided, but not driven, by Christian ideals. Rudolph reports that by the mid-1920s, the president was still expected to provide the primary educational and spiritual leadership for the campus but was also consumed by the necessity of fund-raising and institutional management.[3] This was the situation for Dr. Norton, at Keuka College, who reported of his first year in office:

> During the year [1919-1920] I wrote, longhand (I had no office help whatsoever) more than 3,000 letters, published and mailed at least 10,000 pamphlets, issued a *Book of Views*, made 66 speeches, travelled 16,600 miles...made a survey of 76 colleges in New England, New York, Wisconsin and Missouri.[4]

Dr. Norton was greatly admired by faculty who appear to have acquiesced, willingly, to his final authority. However, like those who would follow him, it was institutional finances which led to frustration and even confrontation with the faculty. Probably the most popular president in Keuka's history, even Dr. Norton discovered that there are limits to faculty's willingness to yield on institutional decisions, particularly when personal welfare is in question.

Expanding Role of Faculty

Throughout the small-school sector, faculty were beginning to play a more important role in decision-making, particularly in shaping the curriculum, as the president was forced to spend greater amounts of his time on fund-raising and institutional management. In the late 1920s, Dr. Norton characterized the changing times for Keuka and all of higher education, saying:

> on the price of progress...Mark Hopkins no longer sits on a log and teaches the boy. Great buildings, libraries, laboratories and endless equipment are now required. A business manager, high-powered money-getting president and a faculty of experts are required. Where ten thousand dollars used to satisfy, a million is now sought.[5]

Even during this early history of small schools, Dr. Norton recognized that the president's role was becoming increasingly external, requiring the faculty to become more active in institutional decisions. In spite of evidence that faculty have a commitment to the general welfare of the institution, research has shown that in the small liberal arts school, there is an even stronger affinity for their own discipline.[6] As such, the changing character of the professoriate provided an opportunity for an over-extended president to begin to view the faculty as a resource which could be used in a variety of new ways. Faculty expertise was tapped to help shape an expanding curriculum in the small-school sector. Professionalization and specialization of faculty was sweeping higher education by the turn of the century, further legitimizing their involvement in decision-making.

Bureaucratization and the increasing complexity of managing colleges throughout this century would also change the relationship between faculty and administration. At Keuka College, the first faculty constitution resulted in the formation of a joint faculty/trustee committee to address various institutional issues. The creation of this committee gave Keuka's faculty their greatest opportunity to influence the direction of the institution without having to work through the president. In retrospect, this action may have been harmful to Keuka as it served to somewhat weaken the president's position at a time when strong leadership was paramount. Keuka, like many other institutions, was developing rapidly throughout much of the first part of this century, expanding programmatic offerings and stretching the limits of its capacity.

It would be shortsighted for anyone to consider Keuka's distinctive development, or that of other small schools over this period of their history, as merely the creation of leadership. Burton Clark cautions that in such an analysis, care must be taken to distinguish between how an institution's distinctiveness is developed and how it is sustained.[7] As an organization, Keuka's distinctive programmatic characteristics were often initiated by the president but developed and carried forth by the faculty. This phenomenon is indicative of the strong core faculty-culture of small schools we have seen illustrated throughout this book.

Modern Challenges

By 1970, private colleges in the United States were in debt for more than 26 percent of the book value of their physical plants, for a total of $3 billion. Nearly 20 percent of all private colleges with fewer than 500 students were running annual deficits of 8 percent or more of their operating budgets, and 16 percent of those with 500 to 1,000 students were doing the same.[8] In spite of popular belief to the contrary, studies have shown that faculty prefer strong and even forceful leadership during such difficult times.[9] More importantly, it was a result of this dramatic shift in fortunes that astute individuals, from both the faculty and administration, were beginning to recognize that their institutions needed a new direction.

Even Keuka's organizational culture, built over an eighty-year period on a foundation of trust, respect, and a sense of security, deteriorated, became fragmented, and nearly collapsed throughout this period. The romanticism of a communal environment, which is so typical of many small schools, also created a false sense of security in their own self-imposed isolation. In spite of this situation, it was still a small core of faculty who should be credited with helping save Keuka from extinction. They did two things in the early 1980s which led the way for Arthur Kirk. First, they took the necessary steps to assure that an individual with the desire and skills to lead Keuka out of the crisis was appointed to the presidency. Second, they gave the new president the latitude he needed to launch the strategic initiatives which would have the most immediate and significant impact on recovery.

Until the late 1970s and early 1980s, there was little to suggest that the faculty of small schools had a formal interest in institutional decisions of a strategic nature. However, faculty have always participated in decisions which ultimately affect the strategic direction of the institution. Traditional involvement of faculty in a multitude of decisions relating to curriculum, academic standards, and staffing reflects the influence this constituency exerts on the strategic direction of the institution. Even more relevant is the fact that these are also examples of the most important internal resources, strengths, and capabilities of an academic organization.

The tendency is to view these types of decisions as elements of faculty governance and not a function of institutional management, which is generally the prerogative of administration. This idea of separate jurisdiction in decision-making has never really worked in colleges and universities and only perpetuates the myth that faculty or administration possesses any absolute authority over matters which ultimately influence the institution as a whole.[10] The reconciliation of our current perspective of faculty governance and institutional management is one of the many challenges which lie ahead in developing a strategic process for the collegiate environment.

In Search of the Elusive Participatory Model

This section will review two sets of principles raised earlier as important elements for an organization to achieve a participatory environment of decision-making. While many argue in favor of these principles, few have discovered the formula for actually implementing them. The following three points are derived from a synthesis of Douglas McGregor's vision of the empowered worker and William Ouchi's social organization, both mentioned in the previous chapter. Together, they provide us with a model for examining organizational decision-making and a means to readily identify the barriers both administration and faculty must overcome to achieve a participatory environment.[11]

(1) Recognizing organizational subtleties: Active participation by all involved.

Careful attention must be given to interpreting this principle. It does not suggest that everyone must be involved. Rather, those who are involved must be capable and willing participants and fully engaged in the process. This distinction in the literature on participatory management is not readily apparent but is one that must be made by all institutions. The presumption that faculty have an inherent right or even desire to be involved in virtually all aspects of institutional decision-making can only lead to chaos. We have seen this problem debated throughout the literature on the subject of administrative decision-making in higher education for many years. Current research repeatedly illustrates that faculty attitudes and values differ along many dimensions. This reality, in itself, precludes any presumptions regarding universal models for engaging faculty in decision-making.

Further, faculty vitality and desire to be involved in institutional decision-making are greatly influenced by their individual perception of reward and recognition. The value of incentives varies among faculty groups and types of institutions. This variability reflects the existence of faculty subcultures in academic disciplines and professional fields, unique institutional missions, and the differential value of incentives at successive stages of careers.[12] The differing institutional perspective of the junior professionally-oriented faculty and that of their colleagues in the liberal arts must also be considered by small schools as their programs continue to diversify.

Within the construct of current thinking on the strategic management process, an institutional imperative to execute timely decisions also makes it unrealistic to involve the entire community. A more productive approach to the engagement of faculty would be to identify both the interest and expertise which can be beneficial to this institutional initiative.

One concern of the above recommendation is that further discrimination of faculty who are best prepared to be involved in institutional decision making can lead to class differences. The professionalization of programs has brought increasing numbers of junior, highly mobil faculty to schools such as Keuka. Such class differences, which primarily cut across programmatic lines, coupled with the

fact that many of these junior faculty simply have less at
stake, makes it difficult for them to act as a unified body.
This phenomenon diminishes the prospect that faculty will
be inclined to naturally unify on institutional issues.[13]

> (2) Organizational climate of trust and mutual
> respect: Effective interpersonal relations exhibits a
> transcending concern with individual dignity, worth,
> and growth, and everyone works towards resolution
> of conflicts between individual needs and
> organizational goals.

This is a critical principle which must be adhered to by
both administration and faculty if a participatory model of
decision-making is to be achieved. The organization's
foundation of trust and mutual respect is based on the
existence of effective interpersonal relations among
members of the community. Increasingly we see this
ideology threatened because of greater emphasis on
organizational efficiency and productivity, two concepts not
always congruent with the slow and gradual process of
building working relationships.

In recent years, we have seen the educational process
slowly transforming itself into one which more closely
resembles the practices of business. Students are considered
customers and faculty are service providers. In terms of
our pragmatic assessment of institutional survival, this
perception seems tenable. However, the institution which
genuinely seeks to discover the participatory model must
also do so within the context of the educational
organization, which, in large part, still has unique
characteristics foreign to any business model of decision-

making.

With the possible exception of the early history of American colleges, the academic environment has generally not worked well as a highly structured and hierarchical organization. When forced to adhere to a chain of command, faculty are more likely to react with hostility than submission.[14] It is also difficult, at times, to determine exactly what constitutes the chain of command in an academic environment. Proponents of participatory management generally turn to the concept of shared authority to avoid such conflicts. This concept, which has surfaced on a number of occasions and in a variety of forms throughout this book, is based on the principles of trust, respect, and sense of shared authority and responsibility. For Keuka and many other institutions, the concept of shared authority and responsibility must be redefined within the context of current realities of managing the college or university.

When the parameters of participation are better defined and articulated, each stakeholder may begin to appreciate, rather than merely tolerate, the role of their partners. Further, trust and mutual respect should not be considered a given in any organization. These qualities of interpersonal relationships must be earned by all constituencies through an understanding that any action taken by an individual should also be in the best interest of the greater organization.

(3) Organizational intimacy: A belief by everyone that a close working relationship depends on acceptance that influence on decision-making relies on openness, confrontation, and working through

differences, rather than coercion, evasion, and avoidance.

Small schools cannot escape the intimacy. The question is whether it is a positive or negative factor in the working relationships among the various members of the organization. At present, it is probably both. While intimacy can lead to unrealistic expectations of each other, the social organization of small schools has certainly played an important role in their ability to hold together during troubled times.

The dilemma for all small schools is how to redefine the social organization given the changing character of the community. The influence of a bygone era are still present among some members of the faculty, and, while it serves to create a sense of pride in history, it also occasionally clouds their vision of the future. This poses a formidable challenge to academic leaders in keeping their institution focused on a common vision and gaining the full support of a diverse faculty.

Related to this perspective of the organization is the character or culture of small schools. Throughout this book, it has been emphasized that the embedded characteristics of the small schools have carried them forward through the good as well as the bad times. This is not unusual for most college campuses, and as some researchers of participatory management have aptly pointed out:

It is ironic that widespread interest in the interaction of culture and management grew out of studies of Japanese firms...traditional administrative practices

> common in American colleges and universities are similar to Japanese management styles...shared governance and collegiality are participatory management.[15]

American colleges have practiced many of the principles of participatory management long before it was a movement in business and industry.

Jean Wyer believes that the academy has simply "turned away" from the collegial model and "its sense of community." In assessing higher education's potential to capitalize on those aspects of its unique culture, she asserts that Ouchi's work has served to:

> remind us of the merits of our own and often undervalued experience and ability...and, instead of explaining how to learn from the Japanese, Ouchi's book could be a description of how American business could learn from higher education.[16]

Perhaps nowhere in higher education is this assertion more accurate than in the small college. In the final analysis, individual prerogatives frequently yielded to the general welfare of the organization.

Future Challenges

On virtually any campus in the country, participatory management manifests itself through those forums where faculty and administration interact on institutional issues. This would include committees, departments, senates, and even the floor of the faculty meeting. What remains to be reconciled is the role of faculty in academic governance and that of administration in institutional management. Where does one end and the other begin? While skeptics may suggest that faculty have lost their decision-making authority on college campuses, this is a gross generalization of the actual situation.

Today's academic leadership also recognizes that for their colleges to remain vital, they must be prepared to manage for the future. The strategic process, oriented towards the future, begins with a reflection of the organization's resources, which defines its strengths and weaknesses, and, thus, its capabilities. Additional studies are needed to provide leadership with a more enlightened perspective of the role of faculty, their most important resource. Just as Dr. Norton and his generation of presidents recognized at the turn of the century, faculty not only have an affinity for their profession and the institution, but they also possess a tremendous expertise. Higher education must discover new ways to utilize this expertise as it relates to the strategic process.

It is a mistake for Keuka or any institution to assume that faculty have any desire to be or even should be involved in all aspects of institutional decision-making. Faculty, like any other resource, are currently deployed to various activities of the institution based on their motivation, interests, and expertise. The actual amount of input faculty have in determining their role varies considerably from one institution to another.

As this study has illustrated, faculty have responsibility for the direct welfare of students and act as caretakers of the curriculum. Both activities influence the strategic direction of the institution. While these traditional faculty roles are widely accepted, less clear is the rationale for involving faculty in other aspects of the affairs of the institution.

AAUP Guidelines are not adequate to provide the needed framework for both the faculty and administration to understand the parameters of their current and emerging working relationship. We are reminded by Keuka's story that the AAUP Guidelines only exist as principles which, given particular situations or individual interpretations, can be largely ignored. It is time to establish more definitive guidelines which take into consideration the complexities and realities of managing the modern college.

Keuka, like many other similar institutions, now considers itself a liberal arts-based college. In its gradual transformation to this status, Keuka has assumed the characteristics of the more comprehensive colleges, attempting to meet the needs of a broader spectrum of the student market. This is a question of strategic positioning, one which not only has implications for the individual institution, but also for all of higher education. For the traditional liberal arts college, future studies should consider the implications of this shift on the make-up and expectations of faculty, as well as leadership, the effects on the character of the institution as an integrated community-- a particularly important aspect of this sector of higher education--and, finally, our current, and limited, perspective of faculty governance.

Thus far we have generally limited our perspective of the leadership role in the strategic process to that of administration. In doing so, we fail to recognize that select faculty can also assume greater levels of responsibility in affecting change. As Keuka's faculty have envisioned and demonstrated in their collective effort to save the institution, they are capable of assuming the role of change-agents.

This requires that we begin to see select faculty in a new intermediary role, one which links the voice of this stakeholder group to the administrative affairs of the institution. In many respects, the advent of academic administrators signaled the beginning of this new relationship. However, even within this traditional organizational framework, the question is frequently asked whether such individuals are representing the interests of faculty or that of administration. It is time to consider new models of academic administration which do not begin with a presumption that the individual must serve only one constituency.

In Summary

The story of the successful recovery of small schools is illustrative of how aggressive and skilled leadership can redirect the limited resources of an institution, provided the faculty are willing and supportive participants. Although not always readily apparent in terms of clearly defined and articulated roles, a partnership does exist in most small schools. It is a partnership based on a common desire to assure the institution's survival.

For this study, considerable time was spent analyzing the history of small schools to portray accurately the influences an embedded culture has on an institution's strategic direction. While an institution's character and strategic capacity are formed over generations of leaders, faculty, students, and many other stakeholder groups, it is through their collective contributions that it survives.

It was not the purpose of this project to provide any definitive answers to the modeling of the strategic process for higher education. However, this study has provided insight into the increasing complexity of institutional decision-making in the small school, particularly as it relates to the strategic positioning of the institution. Finally, the authors wish to make clear that there is no panacea. In our own search for the optimal strategic process and the illusive participatory model for decision-making, it became apparent that no single methodology will meet the needs of every institution. Leadership and faculty, the most influencial stakeholders in the enterprise, must continue to work towards an end which they find mutually agreeable and tailored to their unique environment.

Chapter I Notes

1. *The Small American College: A Vital National Asset* (Washington, D.C.: The Council of Independent Colleges, 1983), p. 5.

2. Alexander W. Astin and Calvin B.T. Lee, *The Invisible Colleges* (New York: McGraw-Hill, 1972).

3. Burton Clark, *The Distinctive College* (New Brunswick: Transaction Publishers, 1983).

4. George Keller, *Academic Strategy: The Management Revolution in American Higher Education* (Baltimore: The Johns Hopkins University Press, 1983).

5. Philip Kotler and Karen Fox, *Strategic Marketing for Educational Institutions* (Englewood Cliffs: Prentice Hall, 1985).

6. *The Chronicle of Higher Education Almanac Edition* (Chicago: The University of Chicago Press, 1992), pp. 56-59.

7. J. Victor Baldridge, David V. Curtis, George P. Ecker, and Gary L. Riley, "Alternative Models of Governance in Higher Education," in Marvin W. Peterson, *Reader on Organization and Governance in Higher Education*, ed. (Lexington: Ginn Press, 1986), pp. 11-27.

Chapter II Notes

1. E.D. Duryea, *Prologue to the American System of Higher Education: Higher Learning in Western Culture* (Buffalo: Occasional Paper Series, Department of Higher Education Faculty of Educational Studies, State University of New York at Buffalo, 1982), pp. 28-31.

2. Frederick Rudolph, *The American College and University* (New York: Vintage Books, 1962), p. 26.

3. Ibid., p. 65.

4. E.D. Duryea, *op. cit.*, p.33

5. Ibid.

6. Frederick Rudolph, *op. cit.*, p. 209

7. Alexander W. Astin and Calvin B.T. Lee, *The Invisible Colleges* (New York: McGraw-Hill, 1972), pp. 13-20.

8. Frederick Rudolph, *op. cit.*, p. 48.

9. Alexander W. Astin and Calvin B.T. Lee, *op. cit.,* p. 20.

10. Frederick Rudolph, *op.cit.*, p. 311.

11. Frederick Rudolph, *op. cit.,* p. 323.

12. Lawrence Veysey, *The Emergence of the American*

University (Chicago: University of Chicago Press, 1965), p. 238.

13. Ibid.

14. Frederick Rudolph, *op. cit.*, pp. 245, 424, 352.

15. David O. Levine, *The American College and the Culture of Aspiration 1915-1940* (Ithaca: Cornell University Press), pp. 59-62.

16. Carnegie Foundation, *More Than Survival, Prospects for Higher Education in a Period of Uncertainty*, (San Francisco: Jossey-Bass, 1975), pp. 25-26.

17. David W. Breneman, *Liberal Arts Colleges: Thriving, Surviving or Endangered?* (Washington, D.C.: The Brookings Institution, 1994), p. 21.

18. Carnegie Foundation, *op. cit.*, p. 28.

19. David W. Breneman, *op. cit.*, p. 22.

20. Carnegie Foundation, *op. cit.*, 104-105.

21. Jean Evangelaug, "A New Carnegie Classification," *Chronicle of Higher Education* 40, no.31 (April 6, 1994): A17-A25.

22. Ibid.

23. Alexander W. Astin and Calvin B.T. Lee, *op. cit.*, p.

93.

24. E.F. Schumacher, *Small Is Beautiful: Economics As If People Mattered* (New York: Harper & Row, 1973), pp. 63-75.

25. Clark L. Dickerson, "The Survival of a Small Private Liberal Arts College: A Case Study" (Ph.D. diss., Indiana University, 1986), p. 7.

26. The Council of Independent Colleges, *Small by Choice* (Washington, D.C.: CIC Publications, 1987), p. 7.

27. Arthur Kirk, interview by Gary Bonvillian, January 1992, Keuka College, Keuka, New York.

28. The Council of Independent Colleges, *op. cit.* , p. 6.

29. Ibid.

30. Burton Clark, *The Distinctive College* (New Brunswick: Transaction Publishers, 1992)

31. Ernest Boyer, *College* (New York: Harper & Row, 1987), pp. 144-146.

32. Lee C. Deighton, *The Encyclopedia of Education* (New York: Macmillan, 1971), p. 496.

33. Neal R. Berte and Edward O'Neil, "Managing the Liberal Arts Institution, A Case Study," *Educational Record*, 61 (Summer 1980): 25.

34. Warren B. Martin, *A College of Character* (San Francisco: Jossey-Bass, 1984), p. 3.

35. Burton Clark, *Perspectives on Higher Education*, (Los Angeles: University of California Press, 1984), p. 122.

36. Robert Nesbitt Hillcoat, "Should and Can the Small Liberal Arts College Survive?" (Ph.D. diss., Wayne State University, 1982), p. 44.

37. The Council of Independent Colleges, *Portraits of Excellence, A Panoramic View of the Small American College* (Washington, D.C.: CIC Publications, 1984), p. 11.

38. Clark Kerr, "Liberal Learning," *Change*, 16 (September 1983): 34.

Chapter III Notes

1. Philip A. Africa, *Keuka College: A History*, (Valley Forge: Judson Press, 1974).

2. Gary J. Bonvillian, "Faculty Participation in Strategic Decision-Making at a Small Private Liberal Arts College: A Case Study of Keuka College," (Ph.D. diss., SUNY Buffalo, 1993), p. 62.

3. Ibid., p. 69.

4. Ibid., p. 70.

5. Ibid., p. 77.

6. Ibid., p. 86-87.

7. Ibid. p. 97.

8. Ibid.

9. Ibid.

10. Ibid., p. 98

11. Ibid., p. 112

12. Ibid., P. 114.

13. Ibid., p. 122.

14. Ibid., p. 124.

15. Ibid.

16. Ibid., p. 125.

17. Ibid., p. 129-130.

18. Ibid., p. 131.

Chapter IV Notes

1. Gary J. Bonvillian, "Faculty Participation in Strategic Decision-Making at a Small Private Liberal Arts College: A Case Study of Keuka College," (Ph.D. diss., SUNY Buffalo, 1993), p. 108.

2. Ibid., 110.

3. Ibid., 182.

4. Ibid., 183.

5. Ibid.

6. Ibid., 133

7. Ibid.

8. Ibid.

9. *AAUP Policy Document Reports*, (Washington, D.C.: The American Association of University Professors, 1984), pp. 105-120.

10. Ibid.

11. Gary J. Bonvillian, *op cit.*, 152.

12. Ibid., 154.

13. Ibid.

14. Ibid.

15. Ibid., 155.

16. Ibid.

17. Ibid., 156

18. Ibid., 160.

19. Ibid., 162.

20. Ibid., 165.

21. Ibid.

22. Ibid., 166.

23. Ibid., 167.

24. Ibid., 168.

25. Ibid.

26. Ibid., 169.

27. Ibid., 170.

Chapter V Notes

1. Edward P. St. John, "The Transformation of Private Liberal Arts Colleges," *The Review of Higher Education*, 15 no.1 (Fall 1991): 83.

2. Arthur Levine, "Opportunity in Adversity: The Case of Bradford College," and R.M. Davis (ed.) "Leadership and Institutional Renewal," *New Directions for Higher Education*, no.49 (San Francisco: Jossey-Bass): 7-12.

3. Ibid.

4. Neal Berte et al., *"Opportunity for Excellence: The Lessons Learned by Five Colleges,"* (New York: Ford Foundation Conference on the Future of the Undergraduate College, March 1985): 16-18.

5. Neal Berte and Edward O'Neil, "Managing the Liberal Arts Institution: A Case Study," *Educational Record*, 61 (Summer 1980): 25-33.

6. Dougles W. Steeples, "Westminster College of Salt Lake City," and D.W. Steeples (ed.) "Successful Strategic Planning: Case Studies," *New Directions for Higher Education*, no.64 (San Francisco: Jossey-Bass): 67-78.

7. Frederick Rudolph, "Consumerism in Higher Education," *Liberal Education*, 79 no.3 (Summer 1993): 4-7.

8. Douglas Lederman and Denise Magner, "What College Leaders Earn," *The Chronicle of Higher Education*, 41 no.3 (September 14, 1994): A25-A43.

9. Jan Krukowski and Woodward Wickham, "Split Image: A Tale of Two Colleges," *College Board Review*, 151 (Spring 1989): 18-23, 37-39.

10. James L. Powell, "At Franklin and Marshall College, Smaller Is Better," *The College Board Review*, no.145 (Fall 1987): 26-29.

11. Carolyn J. Mooney, "Aggressive Marketing and Recruiting Bring a Renaissance to Some Private Colleges," *The Chronicle of Higher Education*, 35 no.19 (January 18, 1989): A13-A14.

12. Bob Finnerty, "Safe Bet: A Job or Cash," *The Democrat & Chronicle*, (September 8, 1994): 1A.

13. Carolyn J. Mooney, "Aggressive Marketing and Recruiting Bring a Renaissance to Some Private Colleges," *The Chronicle of Higher Education*, 35, no.19 (January 18, 1989): 13-14 (Follow-up interview with Vice President of Development, January 1995).

14. James L. Powell, *op cit.*, 26-29.

15. Bob Finnerty, "Hobart-William Smith launch $75 million fund drive," *The Chronicle of Higher Education* (September 14, 1994): 13.

All presidential interviews were conducted in confidence with the understanding that their institutions would not be identified.

Chapter VI Notes

1. Ruth B. Cowan, "Prescriptions for Small-College Turnaround," *Change* (January/February, 1993): 31-39.

2. Ibid.

3. Adam Smith, *Wealth of Nations* (New York: Modern Library, 1937).

4. Hazard Adam, *The Academic Tribes* (Urbana: University of Illinois Press, 1988), pp.1-17.

5. Arthur Levine and Associates, *Shaping Higher Education's Future* (San Francisco: Jossey-Bass, 1989) pp. 161-180.

6. Fred R. David, *Strategic Management* (New York: Macmillan, 1993), p. 24.

7. James Gleick, *Chaos: Making a New Science* (New York: Penguin, 1987), p. 20.

8. William G. Nickels, James M. McHugh, and Susan M. McHugh, *Understanding Business* (Homewood: Irwin, 1993), p. 102.

9. Charles J. Andersen, Debrorah J. Carter, and Andrew G. Malizo with Boichi San, *1989-1990 Fact Book on Higher Education* (New York: American Council on Education and Macmillan, 1989), p. 50.

10. Arthur Levine and Associates, *op cit.*, p.150.

11. Scott Jaschik, "Supreme Court Rejects Millions in Medicare Claims Sought by Universities with Teaching Hospitals," *The Chronicle of Higher Education* XL-44 (July 6, 1994): A34.

12. Scott Jaschik, "Defense Budget Approved by House Would Halve President's Request for University Research," *The Chronicle of Higher Education* XL-44 (July 6, 1994): A31.

13. Karl E. Weick, "Educational Organizations as Loosely Coupled Systems," in Marvin W. Peterson, ed., *Organization and Governance in Higher Education* (Lexington : The Association for the Study of Higher Education, 1985), pp. 42-60.

14. Eugene Ehrlich, Stuart Berg Flexner, Gorton Carruth, and Joyce M. Hawkins, *Oxford American Dictionary* (New York: Avon, 1982), p. 945.

15. John R. Schermerhorn, Jr., *Management for Productivity* (New York: John Wiley & Sons), p. G13.

16. Robert L. Jacobson, "Extending the Reach of the Virtual Classroom," *The Chronicle of Higher Education* XL-44 (July 6, 1994): A19.

17. Alvin Tofler, *Future Shock* (1971); *The Third Wave* (1981); *Powershift* (New York: Bantam, 1990).

18. Alvin Tofler, *Powershift* (New York: Bantam, 1990), p. 82.

19. Philip G. Altbach, *The Knowledge Context* (Albany: State University of New York Press, 1987), p. 66.

20. *The Trustees of Darmouth College v. Woodward*, 4 Wheat, U. S. 518 (1819).

21. James L. Fisher, "TQM: A Warning for Higher Education," *Educational Record* (Spring 1993), Vol. 74, No. 2:15-19.

22. Ruth B. Cowan, "Prescriptions for Small-College Turnaround," *Change* (January/February, 1993): 31-39.

Chapter VII Notes

1. Larry L. Leslie and Paul T. Brinkman, *The Economic Value of Higher Education* (New York: American Council on Education and Macmillan, 1988), pp. 32-33.

2. Pat Hutchins and Ted Marchese, "Watching Assessment: Questions, Stories, Prospects," *Change* 22-5 (1990): 26.

3. Ibid.

4. Jeffrey S. Harrison and Caron H. St. John, *Strategic Management of Organizations and Stakeholders* (Minneapolis/St. Paul: West,1994), p. 4.

5. Michael Parenti, "Power and Pluralism: A View from the Bottom," *Journal of Politics* 32 (1970): 501-30.

6. Hazard Adams, *The Academic Tribe* (Urbana: University of Illinois, 1988), p. 5.

7. Robert M. Murphy, "Management: A Business or Organizational Process," *Army ROTC Newsletter* 9-5 (Fort Monroe, VA.: Published by Headquarters U. S. Training and Doctrine Command, Oct-Nov 1975):5-6.

8. Donald M. Norris and Nick L. Poulton, *A Guide for New Planners* (Ann Arbor: The Society for College and University Planning, 1991), p. 48.

9. Lawrence R. Veysey, *The Emergence of the American University* (Chicago: The University of Chicago Press, 1970).

10. Ludwig von Bertalanffy, "General Systems Theory: A New Approach to the Unity of Science," *Human Biology* 23 (December 1951):302-361.

11. Daniel A. Wren, *The Evolution of Management Thought* (New York: Ronald, 1972).

12. James G. March and Herbert A. Simon, *Organizations* (New York: John Wiley & Sons, 1958).

13. Susan C. Stone, *Strategic Planning for Independent Schools* (Boston: National Association of Independent Schools, 1987), p. 3.

14. Robert Newton, "The Two Cultures of Academe: An Overlooked Planning Hurdle," *Planning for Higher Education* 21(1) (Fall 1992): 8.

15. Philip Sadler, "Management Education--Future Needs," *Education and Training* 30(2) (Mar-Apr, 1988): 21-23.

16. A. Yudof, *The Chronicle of Higher Education* (1992): A48.

17. Maurice Harrai, "Report #1 Internationalization of Higher Education: Effecting Institutional Change in

the Curriculum and Campus Ethos," *Occasional Report Series on the Internationalization of Higher Education* (Long Beach, CA.: Center for International Education, California State University, 1989), p. 1.

18. Russell R. Rogers, "Applying Organization Development Concepts to Higher Education," in Walter Sikes, Allan B. Drexler, and Jack Gant, *The Emerging Practice of Organization Development* (San Diego, CA.: NLT Institute for Applied Behavioral Science and University Associates, 1989) pp. 49-58.

19. Donald M. Norris and Nick L. Poulton, *op cit.*

20. Charles J. Andersen, Deborah J. Carter, and Andrew G. Malizio with Boichi San, *1989-1990 Fact Book on Higher Education*, ed. (New York: American Council on Education and Macmillan, 1989); *The Chronicle of Higher Education*, Almanac Issue XLI(1) (September 1, 1994), p. 7.

21. William F. Massy, "On Values and Market Forces," *Policy Perspectives* 5(1)- Section B (June 1993): 15B.

22. Lee Hansen and Jacob O. Stampen, "Economics and Financing of Higher Education: The Tension Between Quality and Equity," in Philip Altbach and Robert O. Berdahl, *Higher Education in American Society*, ed. (Buffalo: Prometheus Boks, 1987) pp. 107-128.

23. Ernest L. Boyer, *The Undergraduate Experience in America* (New York: Harpers & Row, 1987).

24. Jeffrey S. Harrison and Caron H. St. John, *op cit.*, pp. 5-8.

25. Susan C. Stone, *Strategic Planning for Independent Schools*, *op cit.*

26. Michael J. Dooris and Gregory G. Lozier, *Can Strategic Management Work in Colleges and Universities?* Annual Forum of the Association for Institutional Research Paper. (April/May 1989), p.9.

27. Victor Baldridge and Patricia Okimi, "Strategic Planning in Higher Education: New Tool or New Gimmick?" *AAHE Bulletin* 35 (October 1982), p. 15.

28. George Keller, *Academic Strategy* (Baltimore: The John Hopkins University Press, 1983).

29. Philip Kotler and Karen Fox, *Strategic Marketing for Educational Institutions* (Englewood Cliffs: Prentice Hall, 1985) pp. 9-10.

30. James L. Miller, "Strategic Planning as Pragmatic Adaptation," *Planning for Higher Education* 12 (Fall 1983): 4.

31. Ellen E. Chaffee, "Successful Strategic Management in Small Private Colleges," *Journal of Higher Education* 55 (March/April 1984): 212.

32. Stephen P. Robbins, *Organizational Behavior*

(Englewood Cliffs, 1993).

33. Gregory Moorhead and Ricky W. Griffin, *Organizational Behavior* (Boston: Houghton Mifflin Company, 1992).

34. Ralph M. Stogdill, *Handbook of Leadership* (New York: The Free Press, 1974).

35. John R. Schermerhorn Jr., *Management for Productivity* (New York: John Wiley & Sons, 1993).

36. Douglas McGregor, *The Human Side of Enterprise* (New York: McGraw-Hill, 1985).

37. Willard Zangwill, *Success with People, the Theory Z Approach to Mutual Achievement* (Homewood: Dow Jones-Irwin, 1976) pp. 246-247.

38. William Ouchi, *Theory Z: How American Business Can Meet the Japanese Challenge*, 1981) pp. 5-7.

39. Eugene Fram, "Consensus on Campus: Lessons from University Decision Making in Japan," *Speaking of Japan* (April 1984):20-26.

40. Daniel T. Seymour, *On Q, Causing Quality in Higher Education* (New York: Macmillan, 1992) and Stanley J. Spanbauer, *A Quality System for Education* (Milwaukee:ASQC Quality Press, 1992).

41. Jean C. Wyer, "Theory Z-The Collegial Model

Revisited: An Essay Review," *Review of Higher Education*, 5 (2) (Winter, 1982): 111-117.

42. K. Mortimer and T. R. McConnell, *Sharing Authority Effectively* (San Francisco: Jossey-Bass, 1978) pp. 186-188.

43. Ernest G. Palola, Timothy Lehman, and William R. Blishchke, "The Reluctant Planner," *Journal of Higher Education* (October 1971):494,496.

44. Andrew D. Lloyd, "Involving Faculty in Planning," *Planning for Higher Education* 7 (February 1979), p. 28.

45. Suzy S. Chan, "Faculty Participation in Strategic Planning: Incentives and Strategies," *Planning for Higher Education* 16 (2) (1987-88): 13-30.

46. Martin Finkelstein and Allan O. Pfnister, "The Diminishing Role of Faculty in Institutional Governance: Liberal Arts Colleges as the Negative Case," *Published Proceedings of ASHE Annual Meeting* (March 1984): 4, 5.

47. Carol E. Floyd, *Faculty Participation in Decision Making* (Washington, D.C.: ASHE-ERIC Reports, Report # 8, 1985) pp. 67-68.

Chapter VIII Notes

1. Daniel A. Wren, *The Evolution of Management Thought*, (New York: Ronald, 1972), pp. 209-234.

2. Henry Mintzberg, *The Rise and Fall of Strategic Planning* (New York: The Free Press, 1994), p. 30.

3. Frederick Rudolph, *The American College and University* (New York: Vintage Books, 1962), p. 168.

4. Philip Africa, *Keuka College: A History* (Valley Forge: Judson Press, 1974), p. 109.

5. Ibid p. 142.

6. Ernest Boyer, *College*, (New York: Harper and Row, 1987), p. 237.

7. Burton Clark, *The Distinctive College* (New Brunswick: Transaction Publishing, 1992), p. 256.

8. George Keller, *Academic Strategy: The Academic Revolution in American Higher Education* (Baltimore: The Johns Hopkins University Press, 1983), p. 11.

9. Howard R. Bowen and Jack H. Schuster, *American Professors: A National Resource Imperiled* (New York: Oxford University Press, 1986), p. 140.

10. Carol E. Floyd, *Faculty Participation in Decision*

Making: Necessity or Luxury? (Washington, D.C.: ASHE-ERIC Reports, #8, 1985), p. 11.

11. Douglas McGregor, *The Human Side of Enterprise* (New York: McGraw-Hill, 1985) and William Ouchi, *Theory Z: How American Business Can Meet the Japanese Challenge* (New York: Avon Books, 1981).

12. Howard R. Bowen and Jack H. Schuster, *op cit.*, pp.145-152.

13. Suzy S. Chan, "Faculty Participation in Strategic Planning: Incentives and Strategies," *Planning for Higher Education*, 16, no.2 (1988): 19-22.

14. Donald E. Walker, "Administrators vs. Faculty," *Change*, 18 (March/April 1986),p. 9.

15. Andrew T. Masland, "Organizational Culture in the Study of Higher Education," *Review of Higher Education*, 8 (2) (Winter 1985): 71.

16. Jean C. Wyer, "Theory Z--The Collegial Model Revisited: An Essay Report," *Review of Higher Education*, 5 (2) (Winter 1982): 111-118.

Index

Gary Bonvillian is currently a member of the management faculty at Rochester Institute of Technology, where he teaches in both the undergraduate and graduate programs of the College of Business. His teaching, research and consulting are focused on leading change, quality, and organizational development. Dr. Bonvillian received a Ph.D. from the State University of New York at Buffalo, and has held numerous administrative assignments at RIT, including Associate Dean of the College of Business. His research of the strategic process at a small liberal arts college was the basis for this book.

Robert M. Murphy is the professor of management at the United States War College, where he teaches and researches in the area of strategic management, and leadership. He received an MBA from Florida State University, and a Ph.D. from the State University of New York at Buffalo. Dr. Murphy is a retired military officer, and was assistant to the president for planning and institutional research at a liberal arts college in upstate New York. In addition to his academic appointment, he is an associate with BMK, a firm which specializes in strategic management and leadership.